The Remembered Land

DEBATES IN ARCHAEOLOGY

Series editor: Richard Hodges

The Remembered Land

Surviving Sea-level Rise After the Last Ice Age

Jim Leary

With illustrations by Elaine Jamieson

Bloomsbury Academic
An imprint of Bloomsbury Publishing Plc

B L O O M S B U R Y
LONDON • NEW DELHI • NEW YORK • SYDNEY

Bloomsbury Academic

An imprint of Bloomsbury Publishing Plc

50 Bedford Square	1385 Broadway
London	New York
WC1B 3DP	NY 10018
UK	USA

www.bloomsbury.com

BLOOMSBURY and the Diana logo are trademarks of Bloomsbury Publishing Plc

First published 2015

© Jim Leary, 2015

Jim Leary has asserted his right under the Copyright, Designs and Patents Act, 1988, to be identified as Author of this work.

British Library Cataloguing-in-Publication Data

A catalogue record for this book is available from the British Library.

ISBN: HB: 978-1-47424-591-3
PB: 978-1-47424-590-6
ePDF: 978-1-47424-593-7
ePub: 978-1-47424-592-0

Library of Congress Cataloging-in-Publication Data

A catalog record for this book is available from the Library of Congress.

Series: Debates in Archaeology

Typeset by Fakenham Prepress Solutions, Fakenham, Norfolk NR21 8NN
Printed and bound in India

To my family, with love and pride.

Contents

Acknowledgements

This book started life as my PhD research at (and funded by) the University of Manchester and I thank my supervisor, Chantal Conneller, for support, patience and encouragement throughout. The same goes for my subsidiary supervisors, Colin Richards and Jamie Woodward. Mel Giles and Josh Pollard also provided wise and sensible comments. I am very grateful to all my colleagues and friends who commented on my work at various stages, above all Peter Murphy, Ian Oxley, Zoë Hazell, Clive Waddington, Andrew David, Lucy Farr, Ben Gearey and Hannah Cobb. Special thanks must go to Dave Field for comments, ideas, encouragement and for generally being a constant source of archaeological inspiration to me. I am truly grateful to Elaine Jamieson for improving this book in many ways, not least with her wonderful illustrations. The text was further improved by comments and suggestions from peer reviewers organized by the publisher. I am indebted to Alice Wright and Anna MacDiarmid from Bloomsbury Academic, and to Richard Hodges, the Debates in Archaeology series editor.

Some of the thoughts and ideas contained within this book have been published in J. Leary (2009), 'Perceptions of and Responses to the Holocene Flooding of the North Sea Lowlands', *Oxford Journal of Archaeology* 28 (3): 227–37, and J. Leary (2011), 'Experiencing Change on the Prehistoric Shores of Northsealand; An Anthropological Perspective on Early Holocene Sea-level Rise', in J. Benjamin, C. Bonsall, C. Pickard and A. Fischer (eds), *Submerged Prehistory*, 75–84. Oxford: Oxbow Books.

This book was written in memory of three people from three generations: my grandmother Gwyneth Rowley, my mother Jenny and my brother Piers – you are missed. Finally to my dear family – my wife Ellie, for endless love and support, and our daughters Dora and Aggie, for reminding me of the important things in life.

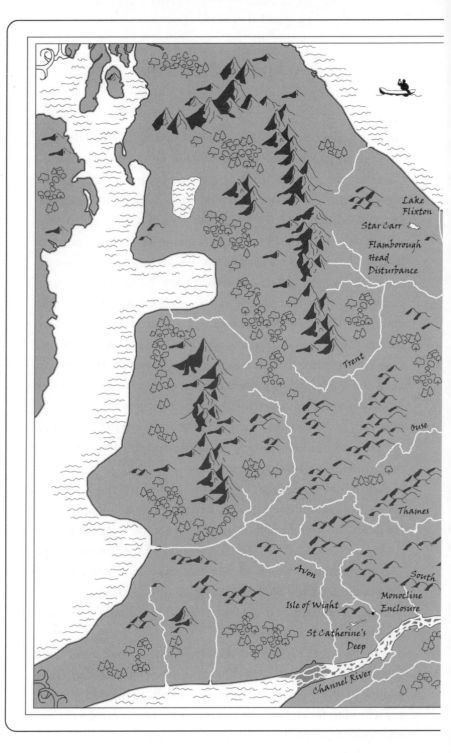

Lake
Flixton

Star Carr

Flamborough
Head
Disturbance

Trent

Ouse

Thames

Avon

South

Isle of Wight

Monocline
Enclosure

St Catherine's
Deep

Channel River

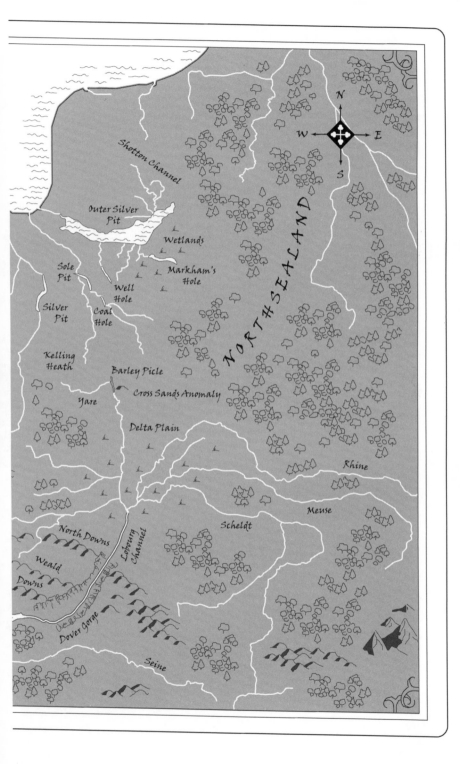

Part One

To Begin

1

Recognizing Northsealand

Sitting in my hotel room in India in 2005, or maybe 2006, something caught my eye on the television. I do not remember the detail or even the programme (perhaps it was BBC World News), but it was about modern sea-level rise and the effect on islanders in the Pacific Ocean. A man, possibly from Tuvalu, was standing in the sea up to his knees, his trousers rolled up to just above the water-line, and he was pointing at the ground beneath the waves and speaking. The subtitles read: 'this is my ancestral land. My father and my grandfather lived here, but there is nothing of it left for me.' That image and his words have stayed with me. A light went on in my head and it made me wonder about sea-level rise in the past: not the recording of it, but the human experience – what it felt like, what affect it had. I have thought about it a lot since and this book is the culmination of those thoughts.

I wanted to write about the processes of inundation in the past, but specifically about how people experienced and responded to it, so I chose the period immediately after the last Ice Age;[1] a period known as the Mesolithic (literally: Middle Stone Age). I focused on an area that was then dry land but now lies beneath the North Sea – an area I shall call Northsealand.[2] The people who lived at this time were Stone Age hunter gatherers who left little trace in the archaeological record. What especially interested me was what happened to their landscape and their lives, and the similarities of those changes to modern ones. The Mesolithic in Britain, as conventionally described in the literature, spans a little under 6,000 years, beginning around 9500 BC. It ended in Britain around 3800 BC, with the introduction of domesticated species and monument building. This is, of course, arbitrary, with some degree of continuity both before and after. The Mesolithic in Britain is usually associated with, and indeed for many defined by, the presence of particular flint implements – little microliths, blades and bladelets. It is also a period associated with, and again frequently defined by, rapid environmental change. The climate warmed globally and as a result ice sheets that had covered huge swathes of north western Europe began to melt. This caused sea levels to rise rapidly and inundate vast tracts of the contemporary landscape. Associated with this, the open, deglaciated landscape changed as coniferous and deciduous woodland developed.

Sea levels have always varied of course, going up and down by as much as 100 to 150 metres over hundreds of thousands of years as Quaternary ice sheets have grown and decayed (water depths in the North Sea are now between forty and eighty metres, although they can exceed 130 metres over deep valleys and channels). Levels are changing still now, increasing at a rate that should alarm us all, and will continue to change, in both directions, in the future. They are, in short, dynamic. The rise in sea levels in Northsealand during the Mesolithic period, however, was a singularly profound process, rapidly altering ecosystems and habitability in coastal regions and ultimately leading to the displacement of communities as land was submerged and lost altogether. What is more, this process occurred exactly where a large percentage of the population are likely to have been located and drawn to, not least for the rich coastal resources, but also for transportation, communication, and for other social and cosmological reasons. Although varying from place to place, the effects of sea-level rise will have caused, at times, severe social and economic problems.

It is not easy setting out to discuss a landscape that is no longer visible to anyone, hidden by metres and metres of water. It is a landscape that no one alive today has walked through. It cannot be seen from the window of the train; it is no holiday destination. It does not have a modern town built over it, and it cannot be easily excavated. No one today can claim that they have come from there, been born there, grown up there. No one is rooted to it in that way. But it was once a landscape of places. These are now lost and with hidden histories. 'It is not down in any map' said Ishmael, the protagonist in Herman Melville's *Moby-Dick*, speaking of the master-harpooner's home, 'true places never are'. Northsealand is a true place. In this age where everything seems to have been mapped and named, there is something stupefyingly romantic about the redis-covery of a truly lost landscape.

This idea of lost landscapes has some heritage to it. 'A very remarkable circumstance occurred' noted Gerald of Wales, the twelfth-century Welsh chronicler.

> The sandy shores of south Wales, being laid bare by the extraordinary violence of a storm, the surface of the earth, which had been covered for many ages, reappeared and discovered the trunks of trees off standing in the very sea itself, the strokes of the hatchet appearing as if made only yesterday. The soil was black and the wood like ebony … like a grove cut down, perhaps at the time of the deluge.'[3]

Clearly to Gerald this was evidence for the biblical flood. By the eighteenth and nineteenth centuries, eminent scientists such as Charles Lyell, Thomas Huxley and William Boyd Dawkins, spurred on by debates over the biblical flood and the age of humanity, took an interest in the submerged forests and landscapes around Britain, and by 1897 the notable archaeologist and geologist Sir John Evans was writing of an isthmus connecting Britain with the Continent. As the British shipping industry reached its climax towards the end of the Victorian period, dock excavations increased, leading to the recovery of peats in the mouths of river ports.[4] These were observed by the British Geological Survey and the findings were published in 1913 by a pioneer of palaeobotany, Clement Reid. Reid recognized them, by virtue of associated finds, as pre-dating the Bronze Age.

Insightfully, he wrote of the submerged forests and peats around the coast of Britain:

> The geologist should be able to study ancient changes of sea-level, under such favourable conditions as to leave no doubt as to the reality and exact amount of these changes. The antiquary should find the remains of ancient races of man, sealed up with his weapons and tools. Here he will be troubled by no complications from rifled tombs, burials in older graves, false inscriptions, or accidental mixture. He ought to here find also implements of wood, basketwork, or objects of leather, such as are so rarely preserved in deposits above the water-level.[5]

Reid deduced that the area now under the southern North Sea must have once been a vast alluvial plain connecting Britain with the Continent, with the Dogger Bank as dry inhabitable land, the size of Denmark, rising up out of the northern edge of the plain. The seventh edition of the politician and antiquarian John Lubbock's *Pre-historic Times* was also published in 1913, and using much of the emerging information briefly discussed the evidence for submerged activity, illustrating the low sea level on a map.[6] Even before this, however, a land connection between Britain and Europe had established itself in the public consciousness, or at least in the minds of numerous school children, when in 1911 Rudyard Kipling wrote of the River Thames in his poem 'The River's Tale' for the school book *A History of England*:[7]

> I walk my beat before London Town,
> Five hours up and seven down.
> Up I go and end my run
> At Tide-end-town, which is Teddington.
> Down I come with the mud in my hands
> To plaster it over the Maplin Sands.
> But I'd have you know that these waters of mine
> Were once a branch of the River Rhine,
> When hundreds of miles to the East I went
> And England was joined to the Continent.

By the 1930s and 1940s the English botanist Sir Harry Godwin was pioneering his analysis of pollen from coastal peat beds (layers of organic material that form in wet environments and are composed of partially decayed vegetation) and using them as indices of sea-level change.[8] In 1931, a lump of peat was dredged from the depths of the southern North Sea by the fishing trawler 'Colinda' between the Leman and Ower Banks. Remarkably, contained within it was a barbed bone point – an elegant artefact that was once one half of a leister or fish spear, and an archetypal implement of the Mesolithic period.[9] Godwin recognized the importance of this find and surmised that it must have come from a time when dry land existed between Britain and the Continent. Soon after, in 1936, the eminent Cambridge archaeologist Grahame Clark completed his seminal book, *The Mesolithic Settlement of Northern Europe*, in which he drew on the earlier work of Reid and Godwin, recognizing the potential that the area of the southern North Sea had as the heartland of an early Mesolithic culture. He did not speculate on the detail of this land or the communities that lived there, but he suggested that the period could not be fully appreciated without considering it; a point he stressed throughout his life.[10]

Despite this early recognition of Northsealand as a heartland, the following decades saw very little research into it. When it was mentioned in the literature there was generally a tacit acceptance that it represented not much more than a land bridge between the two occupied landscapes of Britain and the Continent.[11] It was seen as a passive corridor that allowed people and animals to move on their way from one side to the other, but not an area to live in – to settle, hunt, gather, tell stories and raise children. On top of this, the geographical area of the North Sea, falling outside both Britain and the Continent, attracted little archaeological interest from either side. Clement Reid also accurately predicted in 1913 that 'the archaeologist is inclined to say that [the deposits] belong to the province of geology, and the geologist remarks that they are too modern to be worth his attention; and both pass on'.[12] Northsealand, a Mesolithic landscape larger than the United Kingdom, fell through a gaping archaeological crack. This changed in 1998 when expert on wetland archaeology Bryony Coles published an article in which she discussed the landscape of the North Sea plain, naming it *Doggerland* in recognition of Reid's earlier description of the Dogger Bank rising from the surrounding landscape.[13] Coles challenged the prevalent assumption that the area was a mere land bridge, and – in many ways echoing Grahame Clark – described it as an area that could have supported large populations.

The other thing that hampered research was that the Mesolithic period was frequently seen by archaeologists as the unlovable child of prehistory. The Marxist archaeologist Vere Gordon Childe may be largely responsible for popularizing this viewpoint, suggesting in his book *What Happened in History* that: 'by contrast to what had passed away, the Mesolithic societies leave an impression of extreme poverty'. A point made again in the 1950s by the eminent popularizer of archaeology (and one-time winner of British TV Personality of the Year) Mortimer Wheeler who described Mesolithic people as 'squalid a huddle of marsh-ridden food gatherers as the imagination could encompass'.[14] Mesolithic research is now, mercifully, a far cry from such notions, and the archaeological importance of the southern North Sea in terms of its social and cultural significance has grown no end.[15]

Meanwhile, however, research on the scientific detail of sea-level change had continued unabated. From the 1960s radiocarbon dating of the peat deposits meant that maps showing major coastline changes following the end of the last glacial period could be plotted.[16] These models suggested that at around 10,000 BC the North Sea coastline ran from Denmark to eastern England with an embayment on the west side, which extended further south to Flamborough Head. As sea levels rose, this embayment extended south and then east to produce a shallow estuary south of the Dogger Bank around the ninth millennium BC, while another embayment pushed east along the English Channel, and then northwards past the Dover Strait. This eventually linked with the North Sea via a narrow strait northeast of Norfolk around the seventh millennium BC. In these models, the Dogger Bank was cut off from the mainland during high tides at this time, and by the beginning of the sixth millennium BC was perhaps only exposed at low tide. It finally became entirely submerged by the beginning of the fifth millennium BC, at which time the western margins of the North Sea would have been close to the present coastline. Rapid sea-level rise had slowed down, before oscillating with numerous regressions and transgressions in later prehistory.[17]

One problem with these maps is that their topography is based on the present-day seabed, and this can bear little relationship to actual submerged Holocene landscapes, since major features can be many metres below, and masked by, more modern sediments. Fortunately, significant advances have been made in the last few years in overcoming such discrepancies, particularly by using vast 3D seismic data sets developed by the petroleum industry to explore the deep geology of the continental shelf.[18] Seismic reflection survey involves sending out an acoustic signal from a boat and measuring the time it takes to bounce back. The time taken differs depending on the underlying sediments and therefore allows a profile through the earth's surface to be built up. The data sets have extensive regional coverage and good spatial resolution, allowing parts of the Holocene topography to be mapped in some detail. This can be combined with other sophisticated technologies, such as sidescan sonar (which, incidentally, was used in the search for the missing Malaysian Airline Flight MH370), and less sophisticated, such as coring and grab sampling from the side of a boat (quite literally a giant version of the popular end-of-pier game – the reward being a bucketful of sediment rather than a cuddly toy). It is now possible to see clear three-dimensional images of buried landscape features, such as valleys, river channels, lakes and estuaries, and target these with cores in order to analyse their sediments and look for environmental remains, such as pollen and charcoal. Parts of a landscape lost under the sea for millennia have thus become visible to us for the first time; discarded places once again charted and named.

As well as this, archaeologists have recorded peat beds and submerged forests in intertidal zones around the coast of Britain and the Continent, allowing rises and falls in sea levels to be plotted, providing the smoking gun for sea water incursion. By analysing tiny single celled algae known as diatoms (which are highly sensitive to changes in environmental conditions) within peat deposits, it is possible to observe freshwater conditions replaced by brackish salt marsh followed by fully marine sediments. Peats have been recorded from the intertidal zone as well as offshore locations, such as around Dogger Bank, German Bight, Well Bank, Sandettie-Fairy Bank, and in the English Channel. Submerged forests, like the one seen by Gerald of Wales in the twelfth century, provide tangible evidence for the submergence of once dry land. I recorded a submerged forest once – it was on the banks of the River Thames in Erith, and Bronze Age in date rather than Mesolithic. The tree remains were no more than knee high but were amazingly well preserved, and a Bronze Age wooden track wound its way through the forest. It was both beautiful and eerie to walk through, but, more than anything, just wonderfully evocative. The timing of Mesolithic sea-level rise has been revised and refined by dating similar, albeit Mesolithic, submerged forests, as well as peat from both recent dredging and systematic sampling from cores.[19] Our understanding is ever being added to and improved.

***

So this is something of the historiography of Northsealand, but none of it brings us very close to the landscape or the communities that would have experienced such monumental environmental change. In an attempt to understand this, I jump into my car and drive up to the Museum of Rural Life in Gressenhall, near Dereham in Norfolk, to see for myself the Colinda point; the leister smuggled up from the seabed in a lump of peat by a fishing trawler twenty-five miles off the coast of Cromer. I find it a beautiful, moving piece. A little over twenty-one centimetres long and despite its venerable age of nearly 14,000 years well preserved; shiny, like it is still wet. Delicate notches along one side tell of its careful maker and how it was used. There would have been another identical notched point positioned opposite it and both lashed to the end of a long wooden shaft; together they would have been used to catch fish, probably eels. It harbours stories we shall never know, and yet in my mind's eye I can see the frustration and hear the exclamations of despair as the spear was pulled out of the river to find one prong missing. Importantly though, the discovery of this little object tells us about lost fishing gear, in a lost place, in a land that became flooded, and of a long-gone community. I feel closer now – happier, but still frustratingly distant. What I want to do, what I will do, is head off my island, past the moored modern boats bobbing at the water's edge, and keep going until I reach the Mesolithic.

Part Two

Landscape

2

Thinking the Imagined Land

I like to be able to walk through and surround myself with a landscape to help me understand it. As an archaeologist I like to be outside in the environment, dig in the soil, and feel the weather around me. Often the sites I work on are remote, rural and away from the masses; mostly in the rolling green landscape of Wessex, with views of leafy copses and glinting rivers. And where I can see grazing wethers and hanging skylarks; stonechats sounding like the gentle *chink chink* of distant prehistoric flintknappers. Sounds that, along with the scratching of trowels over soil and site banter, provide the soundtrack to excavations. Not always in locations like this of course; I spent years working as an archaeologist on building sites in London. Even here though I was still outside, with the sky above me, I could see insects crawl and weeds grow in the cracks in the concrete. Pied wagtails lived merrily here – fidgeting and flitting in and out of semi-demolished buildings. I could excavate through the recent rubble to soils from earlier times; digging my way out of the modern metropolis to a pastoral past. This stands in contrast to Northsealand – a landscape unavailable to me, I cannot revel in it. And yet I am drawn to it.

Unavailable to walk through and analyse on the ground, one is left to imagine what Northsealand may have looked like. Consequently, speculating on the people who once lived there becomes that much more difficult. The new and emerging evidence for this landscape, however, does reveal something of the character of Northsealand, which means that we can attempt an imaginary walk through it. The available geological, bathymetric and seismic data are sufficient to be able to identify some key topographical features and main drainage patterns, and combined with evidence from archaeology allow a preliminary characterization of the submerged landscape.[1] Despite this evidence, the archaeological information is, as might be expected from a landscape under the sea, extremely sparse and difficult to date, and the search is always on for the smoking gun. Where sites do occur, their discovery is often serendipitous and information about them tends to be either very general or very local. Any landscape picture (such as the one I am about to present) is, then, broad brush, with much extrapolation, and should not be considered reconstructions in the true sense of the word.

In general terms, Northsealand may be described as a watery, mostly low-lying, flat and fluvially dominated landscape – one that was created by the processes of rivers and streams. The rivers, in most instances, would have cut with relative ease through sands and gravels to form very dynamic and mobile networks of braided channels separated by swamp, reed bed and carr woodland. There were areas of higher land too and the topography was in places varied, but on the whole this was a land of big skies and wide sunsets. At the start of the Holocene, the Northsealand landscape was likely to have been barren tundra crossed by moraines and rivers, much like northern Canada today. The main topographic highs would have been provided by ridges and outcrops of chalk, often representing continuations of the chalkland relief that survives today on dry land. Upswelling salt domes caused by the advancing sea would have formed low hills.

Discussion of this landscape needs to be set against rising temperatures, which allowed the northward spread of warm loving vegetation and animals.[2] In broad terms, vegetation cover is likely to have at first comprised herbs and dwarf shrubs such as juniper, birch and willow. As temperatures began to rise, the late glacial tundra

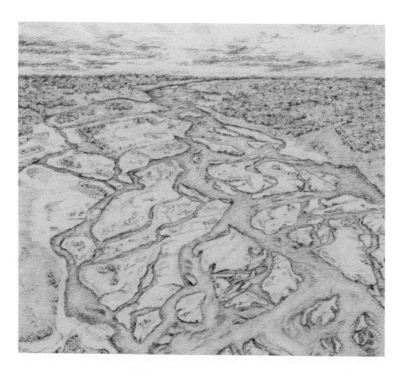

landscape was successively replaced with trees such as scots pine, birch and hazel. By around 9000 BC parts of the area may have been well wooded, with dense mixed deciduous woodland comprising trees that thrive in temperate climes, such as elm, oak, and hazel, with the later addition of alder, ash and lime. Cold-climate herbivores gave way to red- and roe deer, elk and pig. Throughout the Mesolithic period inundation by the sea is likely to have caused forest die-back, creating marshland and tidal flats in the low-lying areas, which would have expanded, dramatically affecting the appearance of the landscape. Estuaries, embayments, tidal creeks and salt marsh developed over these areas as sea levels rose and the coastline pushed inland. This was a dynamic and changing landscape, and these were interesting times.

***

Let us start our journey through this lost world in the area that is now covered by the northern-most part of the southern North Sea: the landscape to the east of the modern British counties of Yorkshire and Lincolnshire. This area lay under the ice sheet during the last glaciation, and as the ice retreated stiff greyish-brown sediment, similar to the glacial till found in the north of England, was laid down over much of the area; this is known to geologists as the Bolders Bank formation.[3] Walking through the area, the first thing that would have struck you is how much of it was low-lying; the main topographic feature being a vast lake, now known as the Outer Silver Pit. This lake measured something like 100 kilometres long and thirty kilometres wide, and must have been an important aggregation place for groups of people and animals. It was surrounded by expansive wetlands and salt marshes, and a number of large meandering river networks, with numerous small tributaries, fed into it.[4] Although smaller, a comparable lake could be the long-vanished Lake Flixton in the Vale of Pickering – excavations around the edge of which have recorded extensive Mesolithic activity, particularly at the famous site of Star Carr. First excavated by Grahame Clark (with whom we have already met) between 1949 and 1951, Star Carr has been the focus of small-scale excavation at various points since. It represents a large, persistently used lakeside settlement dating to around 9000 BC, with evidence for substantial wooden constructions including a large timber platform, and a post-built structure.[5] If archaeologists could excavate around the shores of the Outer Silver Pit now, similar and perhaps greater activity would no doubt be recorded. As a result of sea-level rise, our Northsealand lake was breached, probably around the middle of the eighth millennium BC, becoming an enormous marine outlet the size of the Bristol Channel with strong tidal currents.

If we were to turn and look to the north of the Outer Silver Pit, we would have seen a huge river, over 600 metres wide, with a very substantial flood plain. Named the Shotton Channel by a team at the University of Birmingham, this river valley cut deep into the underlying sediments and would also have been a major landscape feature until eventual inundation. Not all rivers were supersized though: flowing north to south and just south of the Outer Silver Pit (opposite the modern day Wash and Humber estuaries) was a relatively shallow and sluggish river. Three cores drilled through its fill have produced peat deposits that indicate a reed swamp environment fringed by mature deciduous woodland dominated by oak and hazel. This river had disappeared beneath the sea by the fourth millennium BC.[6]

Further topographic features evident across the flat Holocene landscape derive from salt tectonics, and include salt domes – hillocks of a few metres in height, or, where collapsed, a ring of higher ground with a central, probably marshy, depression (known technically as graben collapse). In this flat area, these salt domes are likely to have been visible features and ideal for locating settlements, while the geological strata exposed by collapsed ones may well have been a useful source of flint for tools.[7] High chalk areas evident now on land in eastern England can be traced into the submerged area, around the Wash and further north along the Yorkshire coast. This easily weathered, rounded calcareous topography would have helped determine the nature of vegetation on it. A linear spur of chalk, known as the Flamborough Head Disturbance, extends from the Humber coastline out towards the Outer Silver Pit, forming a ridge of higher ground, and would have also dominated the local topography. Mesolithic activity recorded along the current coastline, for example, at Kelling Heath in north Norfolk,[8] would no doubt have continued into Northsealand, while the major embayment of the Wash, as well as the Humber estuary, would have formed access ways into what is now mainland Britain, but was of course then the higher surrounding land.

Wandering across the landscape, a number of 'deeps' (as they are known by modern fishermen) would have been visible, such as

Sand Hole, Silver Pit, Sole Pit, Coal Pit, Well Hole and Markham's Hole. There is much debate among geologists and archaeologists about how these deeps were formed and there may well be a number of different processes involved, but they are mainly incised into the Bolders Bank Formation and are probably river valleys cut as the ice sheet retreated. This means that they would have been evident as landscape features, possibly as lakes and deeply eroded river valleys, throughout the Mesolithic period until their submergence.[9]

Further south, and beyond the limit of the former ice sheet, the geology is dominated by periglacial windblown sands and gravelly sands, deposited as the ice sheet retreated.[10] The topography of the present-day seabed, particularly off the coast of East Anglia, is somewhat more uneven than the area we have just walked through, resulting from distinctive bedrock outcrops of older geological strata. A feature that would have been highly visible throughout the Mesolithic period in this area is the Cross Sands Anomaly: an isolated flat-topped and steep-sided rock of chalk, located in the wonderfully named Barley Picle channel. Although small, this is Northsealand's Uluru; its Rock of Gibraltar. At 165 metres long, thirty metres wide and thirteen metres high, in this flat area it would have been visible for miles around.[11] This white monolith would have been a known and named landscape feature, likely with spiritual significance to communities in the area. It may also have provided a source of flint, and possibly included cave systems, which could have been used as the focus for acts of formal deposition, or, as with Aveline's Hole in Somerset, the burial of human remains.[12] As the landscape around it flooded, the Cross Sands Anomaly would have, for a period, stood proud of the water as an island, and again was perhaps venerated, much like the sacred Saami island of Ukonsaari.[13] If caves were present, shell middens may have been created within them as they were in caves in the Oban region and Inner Sound in Scotland.[14] How wonderful to think these treasures may await intrepid underwater archaeologists of the future.

The origins of many of the sand banks evident today across the beds of the North Sea and English Channel have not been studied in detail; however, where they have, for example, the Outer Norfolk Banks, they appear to post-date the inundation of the landscape, since they overlie the till of the Bolders Bank Formation and comprise reworked glacial sands.[15] It may be assumed then that the majority of the sand banks are marine features that developed after the land had submerged and would not have been evident in the Mesolithic landscape. Many certainly continue to develop, reworking material as they slowly 'wander' across the seabed, and material dredged from within the Brown Bank includes deposits and artefacts dating from the Pleistocene through to the modern period.[16]

***

Working our way further south now, we would have come to a vast south-flowing delta plain; an area unlike anything else in Britain and northwest Europe today, and, as with the Outer Silver Pit, will have been a key region for contemporary populations. The delta was formed of the Rhine/Meuse river system on the eastern side, and the River Thames on the western, as well as their associated catchments – rivers such as the Scheldt and Yare. Evidence just off the Suffolk coast suggests that the rivers in this delta flowed through a predominantly waterlogged and marshy landscape, perhaps interspersed with occasional open shrub woodland. Cores through a large meandering river channel off the East Anglian coast, probably a continuation of the present-day Yare-Bure valley system, show that the channel was infilled with marshland peat, overlain with progressively more estuarine sediments, deposited as the area was being inundated. A similar scenario can be seen on the continental side with evidence that river channels flowed through an extensive and permanently waterlogged marsh environment.[17]

Further south of this wet and dynamic landscape, the large south-flowing river network, which included substantial rivers such as the Meuse, Rhine and Thames, had, by this stage, converged and amalgamated to form a single thundering watercourse referred to as the Lobourg Channel. This enormous river drained much of what is now northwest Europe and southeast Britain, and the power of it must have been vast, and the sound deafening. The climax of this spectacle saw the Lobourg Channel crash through a gap in a long chalk ridge (a continuation of the North and South Downs in southeast England and which stretches across to France); a gap that we shall refer to here as the Dover Gorge.[18] The Dover Gorge was a major topographic feature, and one that would undoubtedly have been attractive to animals and people. The chalk ridge of the Downs provided a high area overlooking the Lobourg Channel, as well as the large low-lying deltaic plain to the north – the area we have just walked through. This, we know, is a type of location favoured by Mesolithic folk. Between the parallel escarpments of the North and South Downs is the low-lying Greensand Ridge of the Weald; an area well known in archaeological circles for its impressive evidence of Mesolithic life.[19] Just like the chalk Downs, the Greensand geology of the Weald would have continued out into our area.

***

Having left the Dover Gorge behind us we turn west to continue along the same huge river, now running east to west and considerably calmer and quieter. Within this area (the area now under the English Channel) the watercourse is known as the Channel River, although it is sometimes also referred to as the Northern Palaeovalley. This was a substantial and probably braided westward-flowing river some eight to twenty kilometres wide. It continued the Lobourg Channel from the Dover Gorge and subsequently incorporated tributaries with sources in mainland England, such as the Hampshire Avon, Stour, Test, Arun, Adur and Ouse, as well as France, such as the Authie, Somme and Seine.

Structurally the eastern Channel falls within the Wessex Basin, which also includes much of the terrestrial land in southern England. Chalk is extensive across this part of Northsealand; exposed now in large tracts across the seabed. Swathes of Lower Greensand are also evident, particularly around the Isle of Wight, and again, as is evident in areas of Greensand geology on land, no doubt proved attractive to Mesolithic communities. The presence of other softer deposits, such as the Tertiary rocks of the Hampshire-Dieppe Basin, resulted in differential erosion and the creation of lower areas. The ice sheet did not extend to this region, although it will have helped shape the subsequent early Holocene landscape. The area would have been subjected to permafrost and associated features, such as ice-wedge hollows and fissures, periglacial stripes, and small mounds formed of re-deposited chalky gravel from glacial outwash, known as naleds.[20] Naleds would have provided vantage points for hunters, as recorded on similar terrestrial sites,[21] and the gravels exposed by such processes could also have been exploited. The chalk and Greensand within this area probably had similar soils to those found on land today.

The Channel River had a number of tributaries, mentioned above, some of which were flanked by gravel terraces laid down successively in earlier periods. A submerged length of the River Arun has provided rich evidence of an aquatic fen next to slow-moving water with local salt marsh. Pollen recovered from cores drilled through the infill of this river channel indicates that a birch and pine woodland fringed a freshwater wetland and reed swamp during the early Mesolithic period;[22] and this is a likely scenario for much of the area at this time. Surveys of the landscape beneath the English Channel reveal a number of scarps, ridges and high points where rock outcrops are exposed on the seabed. These include the channel margins and bars of the Channel River, and a series of ridges and highs, particularly north of the Channel River around Selsey Bill, west of the submerged length of the Arun, and south and east of Beachy Head. It also includes a now submerged ridge extending from Hengistbury Head (the Hengistbury Ridge) to the Isle of Wight, which would have formed a striking chalk escarpment providing good views across the Channel River. Another ridge, the ten-kilometre-wide chalk Monocline Rampart Enclosure, extends for about twenty-five kilometres from the south coast of the Isle of Wight and would also have formed an obvious topographical marker during the Mesolithic period. Immediately north of this is St Catherine's Deep, a narrow channel cutting more than sixty metres into the underlying Greensand;[23] together these two would have formed dramatic features of the Mesolithic landscape. The most prominent negative feature here is the Hurd Deep, a fifteen-kilometre-long narrow linear northeast to southwest depression. It lies just north of the Channel Islands and would have formed a lake during the Mesolithic period. Another deep is Nab Hole – a three-kilometre by three-kilometre depression to the east of the Isle of Wight.

The English Channel existed as an embayment in the early part of the Holocene, advancing along the Channel River over time as sea levels rose. At some stage in the eighth millennium BC it flooded the Dover Gorge, creating the Dover Strait. As sea levels continued to rise, land was cut off forming islands, the most prominent of which were the Channel Islands on the southern side, and the Isle of Wight on the northern.

***

Having finished our journey, we now hopefully have a better under-standing of the landscape that was inundated after the ice sheets melted. This land will have been a major focus for activity in the Mesolithic period. Far from being an abstract landscape, it was one that was real and, as we shall now see, inhabited.

3

The People of Northsealand

Walking through this landscape in the way we just have gives us a sense of its topography and natural environment, but it feels empty. And yet fishermen and archaeologists have been finding tangible evidence of the people who inhabited this region for some time, the origins of which go back to at least the barbed point dredged from around the Leman and Ower Banks by the fishing trawler Colinda in 1931. Discoveries of animal remains, such as red deer, elk and boar, as well as Mesolithic artefacts, by fishermen around the Brown Bank area have been made from the late 1960s, and artefacts are still regularly dredged from Northsealand to this day.[1]

Astonishing evidence for submerged Mesolithic sites has been recorded along the Baltic Sea coast; and the sites of Tybrind Vig and Fyn off the coast of Denmark provide some of the best evidence for this. Here textile fragments and elaborate wooden artefacts, such as decorated paddles, have been lifted from the Danish sea floor, and well-preserved Mesolithic dwellings, some still with intact wall stakes and bark floors, have been recorded.[2] Similarly, underwater surveys of the Wismar Bay, on the German Baltic coast, have identified a number of submerged Mesolithic sites that were formerly located on freshwater lakefronts or riverbanks. Finds include dugout canoes, fragments of paddles, fishing harpoons in various states of production, and part of an elm bow. In some cases the cultural material is sealed by a succession of mud and reed peat layers, indicating rising water levels.[3] There's that smoking gun.

The construction of the Europoort harbour near Rotterdam in the 1970s led to the discovery of numerous Mesolithic bone and antler barbed points, while submerged sites have been excavated on the dunes in the Rhine/Meuse delta in the municipality of Hardinxveld-Giessendam, The Netherlands.[4] The latter has revealed the remains of dwellings – some with sunken floors – a complete dugout canoe, paddles, elm bow fragments, worked antler, and a fish trap, all providing a wonderful insight into Mesolithic life. The presence of ten million fish bones clearly indicates that fish was on the menu, as were beaver and otter. A number of burials (including, satisfyingly to my mind at least, dog burials) were also recorded.[5]

The Flevoland polders in the western part of The Netherlands have also provided a rich insight into Mesolithic life. The polders (coastal area) of the Province of Flevoland were reclaimed from the sea from the 1940s to the 1960s when the first excavations near Swifterbant uncovered Mesolithic and Early Neolithic sites. It is only relatively recently though, with increased construction activity from the mid-1990s onwards, that their archaeological potential has been fully realized. Many metres below the modern ground surface, Mesolithic and Neolithic sites comprising stone and bone artefacts, burials, structural remains such as fish weirs, and submerged forests have been discovered, all almost entirely undisturbed.[6] South of the Dutch border in northwest Belgium, and sharing the same cover-sands geology, is Sandy Flanders. This is an area, like its Dutch counterpart, rich in prehistoric sites. The river system here was dominated by the Scheldt, which formed a tributary of the Rhine/Meuse delta. The construction of docks around the port of Antwerp in the River Scheldt valley in the last ten years, and intensive and systematic fieldwalking in the last twenty-five years, has led to the discovery of well-preserved Mesolithic sites, suggesting that Sandy Flanders was intensively occupied during the Late Glacial and early Mesolithic periods. Early Mesolithic activity was relatively small and seasonal, probably reflecting mobile groups focused on the banks of river systems. By the Final Mesolithic, activity appears to have been more prolonged with reduced mobility and a greater focus on the lower, wetter areas. These coastal areas were subsequently inundated entirely.[7]

Evidence for Mesolithic activity has been forthcoming from along the Channel margins too, the areas that are today southern England and the coasts of Brittany, Normandy, Picardy and Pas-de-Calais. Numerous Mesolithic sites are known along the south coast of Britain, and developer-funded work has led to an increase in discoveries in northern France too.[8] There are yet to be the sorts of discoveries made within the Channel as in the Baltics, but this zone does offer some potential, and there must be sites – canoes and paddles and houses with bark floors – waiting to be discovered.

Glimpses of this can be seen. Underwater archaeologists working at the base of a submerged cliff at Bouldnor on the north western coast of the Isle of Wight, for example, have recorded Mesolithic period tree stumps (primarily oak) along with worked and burnt flint, a range of worked wood – from a small peg to large tangentially split oak – chippings representing woodworking debris, and prepared fibres, possibly for use as cord, as well as charcoal. This provides a fascinating, if slight, insight into the activities that were being carried out. These deposits were overlain by peat indicating a rise in sea levels, triggering increased wetness and the establishment of extensive carr woodland. The peat provides evidence for a short period of transition from low-lying marsh to mudflat, salt marsh and then fully marine conditions.[9]

A survey of Langstone Harbour – a large, shallow, marine inlet between Portsea Island (on which the city of Portsmouth is located) and Hayling Island on the south coast of England – was undertaken in the 1990s and examined the underwater zone alongside the exposed terrestrial landscape of the tidal basin. This demonstrated the presence of deep Holocene sequences, submerged forests and late Mesolithic artefacts, as well as later structures and artefacts. The late Mesolithic landscape of Langstone Harbour was a lowland basin set well inland, and dominated by two deep ravines that could have provided access from the coast to the chalk ridge of the South Downs; through these, braided and meandering freshwater streams flowed. The dry-land areas supported elements of a mixed oak woodland, while in the valleys open grass and sedge with freshwater fen and alder carr existed.[10]

***

This serves to show that the rich and diverse landscape of Northsealand was clearly attractive to our Mesolithic hunter gatherers. Wetlands, coastal marshes and estuaries are resource-rich environments. They would have been highly valued by hunter-gatherer populations, with easily available freshwater and plentiful wildlife. In fact, estuaries and their fringing wetlands and low-lying hinterlands are some of the most biologically productive habitats on earth. These ecologically important areas harbour immense numbers of microbes, plankton, and other flora and fauna due to rich nutrient supplies, as well as organic matter of both terrestrial and marine origin. These are, in turn, a major food source for creatures higher up the food chain, such as crustaceans, fish and shorebirds, which in turn use the inter-tidal flats as nursery grounds for juvenile stages and as vital adult feeding grounds. This year-round abundance would have been of consequence to Mesolithic hunter gatherers, and rather than seeing Northsealand as marginal space we must understand it as a major focus of people's attention.

As Northsealand's low-lying areas became inundated, extensive coastal shallows were created, which were highly productive of edible molluscs and crustacean, including brown and pink shrimps, mussels, cockles, bivalves and deep burrowing lugworms. We have copious evidence for the exploitation of shellfish during the Mesolithic period, particularly from shell midden sites. Although these enigmatic sites are clearly more than just piles of food residue, since they often contain parts of human skeletons and evidence for other ritual activity,[11] they do demonstrate the collection of, say, limpets, crabs and oysters. Northsealand's estuaries would have also been important for fish species, such as sole, plaice and cod, along with bottom feeders, such as flounder, dab and whiting. Fish that use estuaries as a route from the sea to freshwater, or vice versa, in order to breed would also have been present; eel, stickleback, Atlantic salmon and sea trout, for example. Fish were clearly eaten in the Mesolithic period, and bones of cod, whiting, haddock, pollack, saithe, mackerel and eel have been recovered from numerous sites of this date, while the discovery of fish traps from the coasts of Denmark and other northwest European continental countries as well as from Dublin in Ireland further testify to the value of fish.[12]

Northsealand was an important environment for migratory birds, and water birds attracted to intertidal flats no doubt included brent geese, shelduck, pintail, oystercatcher, ringed plover, grey plover, bar-tailed and black-tailed godwits, curlew, redshank, knot, dunlin and sanderling. Greylag geese and whooper swan would have used this habitat for roosting, and large numbers of Mesolithic period whooper swan bones have been recovered from Denmark.[13] Evidence for the exploitation of mallard and wigeon in the Mesolithic period comes from the island of Téviec off the Breton coast, while bones of the now extinct flightless Great Auk have also been recovered from Scandinavian sites.[14] Seabirds, and their eggs, will have provided communities with an important resource.

Whale and dolphin (or porpoise) bones recovered from Mesolithic contexts in Scotland and Scandinavia provide us with a further understanding of what may have been on their *carte du jour*.[15] Exploitation of these animals may have been opportunistic, taking advantage of beached or dead animals washed ashore, and the gently sloping shores of Northsealand will certainly have been conducive to the occasional whale beaching, while the Channel embayment may have seen whales travelling up it. Mesolithic communities may also have hunted whales, as hunter-gatherer communities, such as the Inupiat in northern Alaska, still do. In fact modern Inupiat communities see whales as more than just food – they use whale skin for drum coverings and whales are a critical part of social life.[16] Seals would have been found in large colonies along Northsealand's coast making multiple kills easy, and both Common and Grey seals were clearly hunted and eaten during this period.[17] Seals are a species in which communities are likely to have engaged with routinely, probably knew intimately, and sealing was no doubt a socially important activity.

Terrestrial animals in Northsealand will have included grazing and browsing fauna, such as deer, elk, aurochs and pig, as well as bear and smaller animals like hare, beaver, fox, dog, badger and hedgehog. These are all evidenced from the Mesolithic site of Star Carr,[18] and some from the seabed itself. As with marine animals, they are likely to have been watched, tracked, stalked, hunted, processed, eaten, related to and symbolized. They will have been understood intimately and thus formed part of the rich economic and spiritual network of Mesolithic life.

Thinking about other resources, Northsealand's wet marshland environment would have provided reeds for basketry and other wickerwork, while flint for making tools will have been abundantly available, exposed in river valleys or the collapsed salt domes, or directly from the extensive chalk ridges. Furthermore, wetlands offer safety and shelter, and often have spiritual or religious importance; somewhere for the dead, for example, as indicated by burials in Denmark, or a place for the deposition of objects (of which more later). Coastal wetlands are also important for transport and communication, and the everyday movement of people via the navigable inland waterways and access to the sea.

***

The coastal zones would have been key areas, and the inhabitants of Northsealand are likely to have identified with the sea and water, and at times profoundly so. The coast has its own patterns and rhythms of movement; ebbs and flows that frequently mark it out as somewhere different. This provides the people, the land and the sea with a distinct identity.[19] Intertidal space, particularly the water's edge, can be a rich transformative zone with distinct entanglements between humans, non-human organisms and the sea. These entanglements also include perpetual and complex rhythms and pulses driven by, for example, the movements of the earth, moon and sun, the weather, seasonal migrations and social life.[20] The coastal zone is a dynamic landscape constantly being eroded or deposited on by the sea. It feels alive; rising and falling as if breathing and sighing. The land and the sea in this area belong together as one.

With shallow waters and flooded land, in certain parts of Northsealand's advancing intertidal zone it may well have been, at times at least, difficult to tell where one ended and the other started. Interactions between people and the sea will have taken place across this margin, blurring any distinction between the two. It was neither just the domain of the land nor the domain of water, but both. This gives the inundating landscape a particular 'flavour', which may have led to groups inhabiting Northsealand becoming distinctive 'mari-terrestrial' or 'land-sea' communities. This may also have made it easier for some to adapt to a fully sea faring lifestyle following final submergence of their ancestral land.

4

Shaping the World with Ice and Sea

We are now beginning to get a pretty good understanding of the landscape of Northsealand, and the people who utilized and exploited it. Let us now think about the processes that caused sea-level rise, processes which resulted in radical change for Northsealand and its inhabitants. During the last glaciation, at its maximum the British-Irish ice sheet extended from the Atlantic continental shelf edge on the southwest, across the area that is now the North Sea to the North Atlantic continental shelf edge on the northeast. It covered all of Scotland, including the Shetland Islands, Wales and Ireland; the ice sheet also covered the area of England north of the Midlands. With water locked in the ice sheets, sea levels were low. As a result of a general warming trend of the global climate, ice sheets began to retreat; the British-Irish ice sheet probably separating from the Fennoscandian some 25,000 years ago. Almost complete deglaciation of the North Sea had occurred by 23,000 years ago, although an offshore lobe of ice re-advanced along the east coast of Britain some 17,000 years ago before retreating again.[1] The ice sheet continued to decay, separating the British from the Irish ice sheet around 16,000 years ago. Following a probable re-advance from around 10,950 BC during a particularly ferocious cold spell known as the Younger Dryas (named after the alpine flowering shrub *Dryas octopetala*), it is likely that ice had wasted entirely from the North Sea area by around 9550 BC.[2]

Water previously locked in ice sheets (as well as glaciers, ice-caps and permafrost) was redistributed throughout the ocean basins.

The influx of meltwater meant that sea levels rose rapidly around the world, submerging previously dry land. The area we are calling Northsealand flooded during this process, eventually forming the North Sea, while the Atlantic coastline advanced east along the Channel River to form the English Channel. These two bodies of water eventually joined; the water thus flowing freely from the North Sea to the English Channel, cutting Britain off from the Continent once again. I say 'once again' because this is a process that had occurred countless times previously as the world went between glacial and interglacial periods.

The mechanisms and processes of early Holocene sea-level rise are complex and controlled by an array of variables, which are worth briefly discussing. These can be divided into two broad categories: eustatic sea-level rise and isostatic readjustment, although there are other things that also come into play, as we shall see. Eustatic sea-level rise is the global return of water to the ocean basins as a result of the deglaciation described above. It has been estimated that the water returning to the ocean basins will have produced an increase of between 100 and 150 metres in mean sea level.[3] There was a rapid rise to start with at an average rate of one metre per century, with peak rates of several metres per century, after which (from about 4000 BC) the rate of rise slowed down.[4] There are, however, many localized variables that modify this rise in global water supply, and vertical changes at any given point are referred to as relative sea level. As we shall see in this chapter, sea-level rise was not a slow and steady process, but a fitful one.

One of the dominant processes controlling these variables is the isostatic readjustment of the earth's surface following the decrease of ice-loads – quite literally the earth's surface bounces very slowly back up when the weight of the ice has lifted after it melts. Imagine a tray of viscous, molten toffee; lay a hard biscuit on top of this and then press gently on one side with your finger (representing the weight of the ice sheet). The side of the biscuit you are pressing on will sink and the other side will rise. And now lift your finger off – the side you were pressing will slowly rise, and the other side, which had been uplifted, now begins to sink. This is happening right now on a grand scale across Britain and certain parts of northwest Europe, and in order to understand the detail and speed of this one has to appreciate the viscosity and thickness of the earth's mantle.[5]

In Britain, uplift centres in northwest Scotland, which was the centre of the former ice sheet, and is now slowly rising, while subsidence occurs in southeast England, which is steadily, imperceptibly, sinking. The 'hinge' line between the two is often placed running from the Lleyn peninsula in northwest Wales, through the Wirral to the Tees estuary in northeast England. Isostatic sea-level change varies regionally, while eustatic change is global in scale. There are a number of other contributors to deformation and movement of the earth's crust, and closely related to isostatic readjustment is the forebulge effect. This is the flexing of the surface just at the ice margin to produce an upward bulge (think of how the toffee bulges up along the edge of the biscuit at the end being pressed), which levels out as the ice melted. The amount of forebulge is determined by such things as ice thickness, ice mass, areal extent of the ice sheet, and thickness and properties of the mantle.[6]

On top of all these processes, the North Sea basin has sunk due to the weight of the influx of water; a process known as hydroisostasy.[7] Furthermore, sea-level fluctuations can be climate-induced, and oscillations (such as the North Atlantic Oscillation) can result in the thermal expansion of ocean water (known as thermosteric), while greater salinity can also result in ocean expansion (halosteric), resulting in regional scales of sea-level change.[8] A further complexity is caused by wind action affecting the motion of the ocean, and which can result in decadal-level variability to sea levels; a process that is still poorly understood.[9]

These are complex processes and unsurprisingly problems still persist in understanding the interplay between glacial isostatic readjustment (the bouncing back or sinking of the earth's crust) and eustatic changes (the influx of water). On top of this the former is typically studied by geophysists, mathematically modelling movements of the earth's surface, while data on eustatic sea-level changes are generally gathered by geomorphologists using cores taken in the field.[10] Complex modelling is used to try to take into consideration all these factors and to understand changes in the relative height of sea level in different areas with varying success.[11]

***

This all serves to show that sea-level rise is a profoundly complex issue. But as we get better at understanding its complexities, and with increased observational data to constrain its modelling, our understanding of the effects, perceptions and experience of past sea-level rise improves. Studies of modern ice melt can also assist with this understanding. These studies clearly show that sea-level rise is not a slow and even process of melting at the sheet edge, but one prompted by dynamic, and at times dramatic, changes. Rapid recent decreases in the size of the Greenland ice sheet due to modern global warming, for example, is not simply meltwater flowing from the surface and ice margins; rather it results from increases in the rate of calving of icebergs. Meltwater penetrates cracks, crevasses and shafts through the ice sheet down to the bedrock, lubricating large sections of ice over the ground and causing them to move, until a tipping point is reached and vast amounts of ice suddenly detach.[12] This has an immediate effect on the sea's level. Such a process also has a positive feedback, resulting in ever more rapid decreases in the ice sheet and associated sea-level rise as a result of increased melting of the ice margin. This dynamic description is likely to have also been the case at the end of the last Ice Age. Sea-level rise was not slow, insidious and stable, which rather implies that it was imperceptible to the individual. Instead, inundation will have occurred in fits and starts, with periods of relative calm followed by rapid flooding as thresholds were crossed and tipping points reached.[13]

Certainly, ice sheet instability is evident from the last deglaciation where a growing body of evidence indicates sudden collapses of the Laurentide ice sheet – a vast sheet of ice that covered much of modern Canada and northern parts of the US. This resulted in large-scale releases of meltwater leading to sudden periods of catastrophic global sea-level rise. These are known as meltwater pulse events, and one rapidly raised sea level by as much as nineteen metres within 500 years, and prompted a return to cooler conditions during the aforementioned Younger Dryas.[14] Another meltwater pulse event occurred a thousand or so years later, this time raising sea levels by around fifteen metres.[15] Similarly, rapid meltwater pulse events from the draining of freshwater lakes dammed by the Laurentide ice sheet are likely to have triggered the so-called '8.2 kya cold event'.[16] This event occurred when an ice dam blocking the drainage of the large glacial lakes Agassiz and Ojibway in what is now Canada collapsed around 6250 BC. This collapse allowed the lakes to flood into the Labrador Sea resulting in a rapid drop in the air temperature, which would have been felt as far afield as Northsealand, and remained depressed for the following 200 years or so.[17] This also resulted in an abrupt rise of global mean sea level; archaeological signatures for which are evident in a sea level jump in the Rhine/Meuse delta in Northsealand.[18] Another event raised sea levels by five metres in the late Mesolithic period over a relatively short period around 5650 BC,[19] abruptly changing atmospheric circulation and 'switching between glacial and interglacial conditions in less than a decade'.[20] Abrupt events such as these will clearly have had an impact on contemporary populations, and should provide a warning to us now.

Other events happened at this time too and will have amplified the impact of sea-level rise. One such occurrence is a story worth telling; an episode that dramatically and irreversibly affected the Northsealand landscape – and one that could happen at a moment's notice again. This is the story of a major tsunami, known as the Storegga Slide.[21] One late autumn around 6200 BC, not long after the '8.2 kya cold event' had begun, a large lump of Norway's continental shelf collapsed causing an enormous underwater landslide, which generated a very large tidal wave. Along the coastal areas the first sign of it would have been the withdrawal of water; the sea level dropping by perhaps twenty metres, followed by the first wave. The size of the wave varied depending on the region and with those closest to the slide being hit the hardest. Along the Norwegian coast, opposite the slide, archaeological evidence suggests the tsunami was ten to twelve metres high, while on the east coast of Scotland it may have been three to five metres high. Deposits from the Faroes and Shetland Islands suggest that the wave may well have exceeded the unimaginable height of twenty metres. Further waves followed; at Greenland four were visible in excavated deposits; at Howick in Northumberland there were perhaps two.[22] The impact of the Storegga Slide tsunami would have clearly had a considerable effect on the landscape and on the inhabitants. These lowlands with their gently inclined coastline, salt marshes and mud-flats were especially vulnerable to the tsunami, the force of which would have funnelled up river valleys. Arguably, it is the regions most vulnerable to such events, the coastline and lower reaches of river valleys, that were the most attractive locations for human settlement, and it has been suggested that 'a number of local bands, or possibly a regional dialectical tribe' may have been extinguished as a result of the Storegga Slide tsunami.[23]

To get back to the point, the key thing here is that sea-level rise, like climate change, can actually be characterized by extreme unevenness: periods, during which little perceptible change occurred, succeeded by major, sometimes catastrophic, changes. Sea-level rise, as with other complex and open systems, is dynamic and non-linear, producing multiple, and essentially unpredictable, effects. In this way, changes are irreducible to simple or single models of processes, and rapid transformations can occur as thresholds are breached and tipping points reached. Changes can happen abruptly at a moment when the system switches; they are dynamic and potentially irreversible.

***

There can be no doubt that the most radical changes to the landscape of northern Europe over the last 10,000 years result from sea-level rise. As ice sheets decayed, sea levels rose dramatically, engulfing vast tracts of land. But this rise is dependent on a web of processes, many of which are still only poorly understood. Sea-level rise is both complex and dynamic. Far from being a slow insidious process of inundation, it occurred in quick, abrupt changes; changes that caused thresholds to be crossed and tipped large systems over the edge. These processes of change unfolded on a local scale; they were perceived locally and formed part of everyday life. And we should remember that although we now know sea-level rise to have been a global phenomenon with a long chronology, it would not have been understood as such by Mesolithic communities; the changes would have been experienced within living time.

Part Three

Effects

5

Changing Worlds

Genes may be said to be the building blocks of life, but it is our environment that really makes us who we are. From the moment we are born it pours into our bodies through the air we breathe, and floods us with sights and sounds and smells. We feel the mud under our feet, which squelches up and between our toes and under our nails, and we soak up the warm summer sun through our skin. Nature is not separate; not a backdrop against which life occurs – it is life. And the world around forms us, just as we shape it. Our bodies and our environment are indivisible, and together they fashion the fibre of our being.

In the following two chapters I will turn to the effects of sea-level rise in Northsealand, showing how organisms (including people) and their environments are fundamentally connected through a complex network of interactions, from the biological to the physical, and from the smallest to the largest. Minor changes can lead to major consequences, many of which are subtle, complex and difficult to predict. Throughout these chapters I will keep the focus on the human perceptions and consequences of the changes brought about by sea-level rise, and show that environmental change was not external, not a force 'out there' to fight against, but an inseparable part of a person's life.

Coastal systems are dynamic, complex and non-linear, and small changes can have large implications. Environments are constantly changing, and we should not assume that Northsealand was in any way 'stable' prior to sea-level rise. Considered here, however, are the periods of rapid sea-level rise; the rise that would have occurred during and following, for example, the meltwater pulse events described in the last chapter. The changes that occurred during these periods were perceptible – not just across generations but within human lifetimes. Relative sea-level rise has the potential to trigger a wide range of physical effects on ecosystems. Five main categories of landscape change due to sea-level rise have been identified in the climate change literature, so let us start with these.[1] They are: submergence and loss of land, erosion of deposits, increased flooding and storm damage, saltwater intrusion into aquifers, and rising water tables. To these I will add: changing tidal regimes, changes to river dynamics and estuary morphology, reduced territory, the loss of sources, such as flint, and small island vulnerability.

Of course not all communities living in Northsealand would have been equally affected by sea-level rise; they would not have been uniformly exposed to the changes, nor had the same resources to deal with them. Some communities would have been located further from regions affected by sea-level rise, while others would have been directly, and perhaps drastically, affected. The changes would have differed even in neighbouring areas, since coastlines vary greatly between localities; and so while a beach shoreline may be submerged by sea-level rise, a cliffed coast may be eroded and become dangerous and unstable. The local scale is important. What is more, differences between separate sectors of the community have the potential to highlight social disparities, perhaps serving to reveal previously hidden tensions between genders, classes, castes or age groups. There may also have been tensions between those communities affected by rapid sea-level rise and those living beyond its reach.

***

Let us get the most obvious consequence out of the way first: greater sea-level rise meant the submergence and loss of land. The speed of this process would have mainly been a function of the topography, with the smaller the slope gradient the greater the rate and extent of inundation. In a largely low-lying and flat landscape like Northsealand submergence is likely to have been, in general terms and with some obvious exceptions, a rapid process. Inundation would have resulted in higher water tables and boggy soils, as well as the invasion of salt-tolerant plant species, known as halophytes, and the development of salt marshes.[2] Salt marshes grow vertically by producing biomass and depositing sediment, and can generally keep pace with slow sea-level rise. But where the rate of sea-level rise exceeds the threshold for this to occur, as clearly happened in Northsealand, plants become waterlogged and the marshes are not able to accrete fast enough, causing the ecosystem to rapidly collapse and the land to drown.[3] Given the low-lying nature of topography evidenced from much of Northsealand, submergence would have been a perceptible process as thresholds were reached. This is certainly the case in the Rhine/Meuse river mouth in the middle to later seventh millennium BC where a rapid change from extensive wetlands to a coastal and estuarine environment is evident.[4]

As we have seen, these low-lying ecosystems are important wildlife refuges, particularly for birds, as well as serving as vital fish and shellfish nurseries, and were valued by Mesolithic communities; such habitat loss affected the distribution of a wide variety of taxonomic groups. Species respond individualistically to environmental changes through shifts in distributional range, and these shifts include emigration, local extinction, or immigration and colonization by a new species – impacting upon the composition and structure of communities. Modern sea-level rise in the English Channel, for example, has significant consequences for the transport and population connectivity of marine organisms with a planktonic larval phase, significantly affecting patterns of distribution, and thus the surrounding food web.[5] Removing 'keystone' species from an environment can have large implications for the biodiversity, stability and overall resilience of the ecosystem. In Northsealand, submergence of parts of the landscape brought profound changes to the nature and distribution of birds, animals (including sea mammals) and vegetation.[6] Some species will have increased in numbers while others decreased or disappeared altogether. The changing availability of vegetation would have led to a shift in the behaviour and migration routes of animals, such as deer, attracted by richer vegetation for forage and refuge, as well as their selection of calving grounds, while traditional migration routes became blocked and inaccessible due to submergence of land and changes to river systems. There would also have been incidences of different species – new arrivals, as environments changed. These, no doubt, offered new resource opportunities, which would have been quickly exploited by humans. Such changes, though, would inevitably have put pressure on established subsistence activities and overall productivity, possibly leading to changes in traditional hunting grounds.

Furthermore, as ground-water tables in areas adjacent to the coast rose, ponding occurred, drowning the trees and producing swathes of dead woodland. As we have seen, the stumps of trees killed and submerged in this way have been widely recorded at coastal and intertidal sites around Britain. But let us give some consideration to the significant loss that forest die-back imposed on local communities; from firewood and timber for building or renewing houses, trackways, boats, tools and other purposes, to the loss of plants – some perhaps important foodstuffs, others medicinal or totemic or sacred. Marine incursion affects soil microbes and fungi, which are strongly linked to plant survival and fecundity. Habitat loss would have led to the local extinction of organisms, reducing carrying capacity and thus species richness. Additionally, there would have been the loss of woodland animals, such as wild pig, deer and elk, which will have moved on when the ground became waterlogged, and when there were no green woodland shoots to graze on or leaves to provide camouflage. Woodland birds will also have deserted the area, unable to feed on berries or hunt mice and other small prey. As woodlands died and land submerged, the whole environment irreversibly altered, and with it fundamental perceptions, understandings and interpretations of place (we will come to these in the next chapter).

Submergence of the landscape not only modified its visual appearance, but its effects on other senses as well; for example, the acoustic profile of a place will have changed according to the varying proximity of a body of water. In this way the characteristic and familiar sound of a place may be different following inundation, challenging the very way a place is perceived and appreciated. The same is true of light, which also changes with proximity to water – think of the large numbers of artists who congregate in, for example, St Ives in Cornwall or Staithes in North Yorkshire in the UK.

It is also worth reflecting on how the recently submerged land, particularly the dead woodlands, may have been viewed. They may have been a harbinger of further flooding; an indication of sea encroachment, but they will have been eerily quiet, devoid of leaves, growth and much of the life that once dwelt amidst them. It is possible that mythologies grew up to explain this phenomenon – perhaps dead woodlands became taboo areas or lands of the spirits; perhaps even the association with silence and death led to burials being located in submerging areas. Canoeing through the Amazon flood plain, one anthropologist noted: 'we fell silent as we entered the flooded forest. Indeed, it seemed to demand veneration. The trees were like pillars in a church so that it seemed we were moving through a watery nave.'[7]

***

Another process integral to sea-level rise is erosion of deposits, and in particular of sandy beaches. Settlements on the aeolian sand-dunes in the Rhine and Meuse river areas, such as Hardinxveld-Giessendam in The Netherlands, which were occupied in the sixth and fifth millennia BC, or the persistently occupied sites on dunes in Sandy Flanders would have been particularly vulnerable to erosion. Higher sea levels accelerate shore retreat by causing erosion further up the beach profile, with waves breaking closer to the shore, while long shore sediment transport is also increased due to deeper water. This process is explained by the Bruun erosion model which proposes that higher sea levels cause sediment to be removed from the nearshore area and deposited in the lower part of the beach profile, allowing occasional high-energy waves (such as from storms) to attack further up the beach.[8] Recent research on modern sea-level rise suggests that open-ocean sandy beaches erode at a rate that averages somewhere between fifty and 150 times the rate of sea-level rise. So, for example, a sea-level rise of 3.5 mm a year at the beach resort of Ocean City, Maryland translates into five metres of beach erosion every decade, requiring a continuous programme of 'beach nourishment' (a euphemism for importing vast amounts of sand) to keep it in recreational use.[9] In this way, erosion will be considerably greater than the actual sea-level rise itself. While shores are highly dynamic, it is clear that sea-level rise would have increased erosion, particularly of sandy deposits, changing the shape and location of the shoreline and any occupied dune sites.

***

Flooding is a normal phenomenon in coastal zones; however, it increases as a result of sea-level rise, particularly in low-lying areas where it is a prelude to submergence. The loss of protective sand beaches described above and the erosion of natural coastal systems such as wetlands, combined with submersion, removes natural defences and amplifies flood hazards. This increases the exposure of coastal human communities to extreme events such as storm surges and tidal waves.[10] This would have had an effect on Northsealand's coast, particularly when a critical threshold, such as a natural levee, was overtopped, rapidly inundating the land, and causing an irreversible process of drowning. Further, the breaching of coastal barriers, such as coastal headlands, as a result of floods and storms would allow propagules of intertidal species to move rapidly into new communities, changing ecosystems.

As well as the immediate physical risks to people associated with severe flooding (such as direct physical injury, and, depending on the speed of flooding, possible drowning), other health risks include an increased likelihood of waterborne diseases. Human and animal waste and animal carcasses can be washed into water supplies, causing diarrhoeal disease.[11] Although perhaps a function of more settled communities, there are increased reports of cholera following flood events, while Leptospirosis, transmitted from the urine of an infected animal, is also associated with enhanced flooding.[12] Some vector organisms (for instance, mosquito populations) can also increase following floods due to the presence of stagnant or slow-moving water, or through ponding as a result of rising water tables; others (such as ticks) multiply with increased rainfall. Incidences of malaria are likely to have increased with the extension of waterlogged and marshy zones, and parts of Northsealand may have become 'no-go' or 'taboo' areas as a result.[13]

There is a strong association between sea-level rise and an increased intensification of extreme events, such as storms and surges. This in turn leads to flash-flooding and rapid loss of ecosystems. More frequent wind storms would have led to heavier wave action, thus increasing the deterioration of the shoreline and associated ecosystem loss. Changes in the extent of sea-ice during deglaciation will have also affected wave behaviour, changing the fetch over which the wind was blown, and perhaps increasing wave action.[14] Throughout the historic period, surges driven by mid-latitude storms have resulted in significant damage and loss of life in the area of the southern North Sea. This includes a devastating storm surge in 1953, and an earlier and even more dramatic one in the Bristol Channel and Severn Estuary in 1607,[15] and some models predict an increase in the height of future storm surges as a result of modern climate change.[16] An increase in the frequency of extreme events, such as storm surges, would have had significant implications for intertidal organisms, particularly the very little macrobenthos. Just to take an example, it has been documented how after a catastrophic flood event in the southwest of the United States there was a wholesale reorganization of a rodent community, with a complete change in the dominant species.[17] This shows how a perturbation can entirely and irreversibly change the outcome of ecological processes, and sometimes in the most unexpected of ways; in effect, it re-sets the ecosystem. Major storms can also clear tracts of woodlands and damage infrastructure, such as houses, trackways, platforms, fish traps and so on.

In the Mesolithic period, increases in storm events would have made conditions less predictable. Travel and hunting will have become more difficult, since it increases the chances of being caught out in a storm or getting lost. Stronger winds and more violent wave motion on the coast will have resulted in dangerous boating conditions, causing a drop in hunting and fishing opportunities.[18] Rougher waters may also have led to fewer seals around Northsealand's coastline and perhaps changed fish and seal migrations. It will also have affected fish migration upstream, such as that of salmon, upsetting the location and timing of harvesting.

***

As sea levels rose, saltwater would have intruded into coastal surface waters and freshwater aquifers and penetrated along rivers, contaminating them and making them unusable for drinking water. Its landward reach would have been further extended by storm surges or other high-energy events, shortening the rivers and removing resources. Freshwater lakes within Northsealand were breached by the sea, and this would have had the effect of killing the fish and rendering the lake water undrinkable. Think of the impact of marine incursion on a substantial lake such as the Outer Silver Pit; this is likely to have been a central node attracting aggregations of people, and perhaps with an abundance of sites surrounding it. Saltwater intrusion has a profound impact on coastal communities, affecting individuals' health and making it a challenge to find sources of drinking water. As Henry Chu put it when discussing recent sea-level rise in Bhamia, Bangladesh:

> Global warming has a taste in this village. It is the taste of salt. Only a few years ago, water from the local pond was fresh and sweet on Samit Biswas' tongue. It quenched his family's thirst and cleansed their bodies. But drinking a cupful now leaves a briny flavour in his mouth. Tiny white crystals sprout on Biswas' skin after he bathes and in his clothes after his wife washes them.[19]

Along the coastal zone the abundance, distribution and diversity of intertidal macrofauna in estuaries would have been severely affected by salinity, impacting on higher trophic levels, such as fish, shorebirds and humans. It is likely that increased salinity would have caused a major decline of oyster beds in the later Mesolithic. Similarly it has been suggested that a decrease in salinity through the process of isostatic uplift can be detected by the virtual disappearance of oysters from Ertobølle middens in Scandinavia. Such an ecological crisis, goes this particular argument, would have led directly to the adoption of farming.[20] Any shift in salinity will severely affect the vegetation communities fringing the coastal areas through penetration of saltwater into the fresh ground-water table.

***

The effect on the tidal regime when the North Sea and Channel embayment finally linked would have been significant. It would have resulted in chaotic tides initially and a disruption of the food chain that may have significantly impacted on people living off marine sources in the area. Palaeotidal modelling suggests that as the two seas met, there would have been a rapid increase in tidal range, which would have penetrated far inland through the river networks.[21] Certainly, the disruption to the food chain would have been considerable, affecting plankton, fish and shellfish populations and other marine organisms. This, in turn, would have influenced and changed people's diets. Further, the consequences would have rippled deep inland through extended tidal ranges along rivers.

***

Another effect of sea-level rise is the changes that would have taken place to rivers and estuaries. Rivers will have been shortened and eventually disappeared altogether as sea-levels rose, and not only would this have had an impact on human territory size (we will come to this next), but also on the availability of freshwater. Rising sea level would also have resulted in morphological changes to the coast, particularly estuaries, due to increased water depth and enhanced wave and tidal energy. These include coastal steepening and the removal of finer sediments leading to higher tidal levels. Increased sedimentation as a result of lower river flow velocities would also have had important consequences for the courses of rivers, changing and bifurcating them and raising riverbed levels. In turn this would have led to further changes upstream, extending the landward impact of sea-level rise. These alterations change their physical appearance. Small eyots appear and disappear with little notice, creating a shifting, disorientating landscape.

While an estuary may re-establish its original structure further upstream, changes to salinity, tidal energy, sediment size and intensified siltation rates would have an immediate impact on the organisms within the areas affected, resulting in significant biological loss. Species richness, abundance and biomass of present-day invertebrate assemblages are strongly affected by physical changes to the ecosystem, and this in turn affects the estuarine food webs. Archaeological evidence for this has been suggested at the Mesolithic and Neolithic shell midden at Norsminde in Denmark, where increased sedimentation is suggested as a cause for a decrease in the size of oysters.[22]

Changes to freshwater inflows into estuaries further alter the system, resulting in significant effects on, for example, phytoplankton populations and fish nurseries. An increase in water temperature could affect algal production, and therefore the availability of light, oxygen and carbon for other species.[23] This would have significantly impacted on the abundance and biomass of all organisms, from the microscopic level to the consumers they support, such as fish, shrimps, shorebirds and people. Further, changes to the environment influence numerous aspects of fish physiology and ecology; for example, behavioural responses of fish have been shown to include migration and changed activity patterns.[24]

***

The reduction of the length of river valleys as estuaries were pushed inland, as well as the loss of land in the coastal regions due to the processes already described, would have had a major effect on human territory size and must have required a reconfiguration of mobility patterns. In Northsealand, entire river systems such as the Channel River, Shotton River and others around the Outer Silver Pit were lost through this process. This will have affected a substantial proportion of the inhabitants, since activity is likely to have focused along river valleys. Loss of land as a result of sea-level rise will have caused a 'coastal squeeze' with some people forced ever further inland, possibly along river systems, placing greater pressure on the remaining landscape.

Long-lived Mesolithic buildings such as the ones excavated at Howick in England, East Barns in Scotland and Mount Sandel in Ireland may indicate a greater territoriality,[25] and we can well imagine that a result of the loss of land will have been increased tensions and warfare. Certainly it has been argued that the Chumash maritime hunter fisher gatherers in California increased warfare during the Medieval Climatic Anomaly as a result of resource shortages.[26] In the Mesolithic, such pressures are likely to have increased tensions and led to greater violence between communities, and human remains from cemeteries at Skateholm and beyond suggest some people were certainly the victim of increased violence.[27]

Reduced territory, crowding and increased social engagement may similarly have led to social intensification. Let us not forget though that social tensions can lead to the development of subcultures (grouped by things like religion, ethnicity and sexuality), which can flourish and enrich social lives more broadly. Not all effects were entirely and necessarily negative.

***

Another important aspect of the inundation of Northsealand was the cutting off and loss of important flint sources as they became submerged. In the Vale of Pickering in North Yorkshire, the Long

Blade sites of the Pleistocene/Holocene transition employed good-quality glacial till material presumed to have been collected from a source somewhere in the now drowned North Sea plain. However, by the early Mesolithic, lower quality beach pebble was used for tool manufacture, most probably as a result of the inundation of the original flint source.[28] A similar situation may be argued for the southwest peninsula of Britain where there is a change from larger, high-grade translucent flint in the earlier Mesolithic to the use of smaller beach pebbles in the later. Further shifts in raw material use come from the exploitation of Blackdown chert in Somerset, which appears to be only locally used in the early Mesolithic but more widespread later on, perhaps as other sources became cut off.[29] In this context, it is interesting to note the shift in use from Wommersom quartz in the early Mesolithic to Tienen quartz in the middle Mesolithic in Sandy Flanders.[30] This is a situation that may well be true for many of the North Sea coastal sites, and more work is required to analyse the chemical signatures of tools used on coastal Mesolithic sites to identify possible source materials.

Flint sources have been linked to particular tool types, and people evidently travelled to specific locales to select stone appropriate for use. Therefore removing a flint source, which would have been valued for its physical, symbolic and other properties, may have significantly disrupted the process of tool manufacture, obligations, social duties, ontologies and life ways. The higher chalk areas of Northsealand, for example, off the Yorkshire coast, or the chalk upland around the Dover Gorge, or in the eastern Channel, like their (what is now) terrestrial counterparts, would have been flint-bearing and potentially of great importance in the early Holocene. High-quality flint from the chalk between the later flint mines of Cissbury in Sussex and Jablines and Spiennes on the Continent may have been particularly valued.

***

Small offshore islands that were formed as the low-lying areas flooded would have been particularly vulnerable to even small rises in sea level. While small islands would have varied, all the above described effects – land submergence, beach erosion, increased storm flooding, higher water tables, salinity intrusion and overall reduced freshwater supply – would have been profoundly felt. Eventually these islands were lost altogether and, where occupied, would have resulted in migration off the island. They would also have been particularly susceptible to hazards, such as the Storegga Slide tsunami, due to their small size, limited range of natural resources, narrow biological diversity, relative isolation, and extensive land–sea interface. Greater vulnerability and an insularity and remoteness of human groups on such islands will have created a feeling of marginalization.

***

Perception is clearly a key factor for how people understood changes. But perception is a complex sensory process, and develops gradually through a person's social and cultural background, education, experience, observation, understanding and knowledge over a lifetime. While sea-level rise is a long-term process, and erosion of beaches may have a lag-time, submergence, flooding and saltwater intrusion have an immediate effect. In fact, many of the effects described would have occurred at a human scale, within an individual's lifetime; they would have been seen and felt. Indeed submerged tree stumps provide powerful and evocative evidence for the rapid submergence of land. Describing the loss of land during the Mesolithic simply as an 'inundation' actually misses the human impact.

The different effects of sea-level rise would have been perceived at different levels and rates. In a study of the impact of modern sea-level rise on farmers in Maheshkhali on the southeastern coast of Bangladesh, for example, overflow by high tides and storm surges, as well as salinity contamination of the soil and ground water, are the most easily observed effects of sea-level rise, with most respondents in the study having witnessed them.[31] Over half also noticed a decline in animal populations, probably largely the result of more frequent natural disasters. Similarly, in a study of farmers in the Limpopo River Basin, South Africa, about 95 per cent of the interviewed farmers perceived long-term changes in temperature and 97 per cent perceived changes in rainfall over the last twenty years.[32] So we can see that many of the changes that occurred in Northsealand were likely to be perceptible, and were occasionally catastrophic.

Not all communities living in the North Sea basin were equally affected by flooding, and clearly different settlements and landscapes would be differentially susceptible, with the most affected and particularly vulnerable areas being coastal dunes, coastal wetlands, estuaries and small islands. The effects of sea-level rise cannot be easily summed up or characterized; it was highly variable, playing out in different areas in different ways and over a variety of timescales. Further, differences between people, behaviour, topography, technology, and access to resources such as water, would have led to different adaptations and coping strategies; local-scale differences, including things such as gender, age and disabilities, must be stressed. While the changes discussed in this chapter are physical in nature, they have been approached by constituting the human and non-human world together. People were not detached entities existing separately from the landscape; they were integrally linked.

6

Losing Place

The landscape provides identity to people and communities. Human lives are enmeshed with place, and people are embodied and located. When places are removed through, say, inundation, so is a person's sense of place in the world. This is the other side of sea-level rise; that is, the loss of place for inhabitants as the landscape flooded. When Northsealand landscapes changed and disappeared it was not simply a backdrop that went – something that could be re-created elsewhere. It was a landscape that was alive, that had a past, both mythical and historical, and was inscribed with paths and places that were meaningful to the people who lived within them. Northsealand represented a storehouse of memories and ideas, and narratives were written into it.

Place is evocative; it can remind us of an earlier event, a feeling, a person, a loved one, a death, or an experience from childhood; it is closely tied to memory. Every woodland glade, coppiced tree or axe mark, and every flint scatter or decaying house platform in Northsealand told of a history – both personal and communal; a story of actions past and of lives lived in that place. The eminent anthropologist Keith Basso claimed of the Western Apache of the US Southwest that 'because places are visually unique (a fact marked and affirmed by their possession of separate names) they serve as excellent vehicles for recalling useful knowledge'.[1] In this way, features in the Western Apache landscape are descriptively named and tied to lifeways, providing a sense of place and history. This is true of most hunter-gatherer groups, and can be seen, for example, from Saami culture and other northern Eurasian small-scale groups, to Inuit groups.[2]

The Northsealand landscape would have been imbued with meaning. The sites in the Flevoland polders or Sandy Flanders, or the scatters of flint dredged up from the depths of the North Sea by trawlers, indicate places – locations, where lives were acted out by people who would have had an intimate knowledge of that area. They were places that invoked memories, and people were attached to them. They no doubt had special significance for family histories, for kinship ties, and held meaningful, emotional memories for descendants. Many of the natural features too, such as the Cross Sands Anomaly, the Outer Silver Pit or the Dover Gorge, were potentially wrapped up in myths and stories. Equally, they may have been considered animate and fundamental to the myths and origins of people; perhaps thought to be places where the spirits dwelt; or even the physical manifestation of powerful deities. They would have had stories and memories attached to them and been the focus of songs; places where an individual's parents were killed, or where they were initiated, or where some other significant life event had once occurred. Others would have been traditional hunting grounds connected by a network of paths and travel routes. Such places provided a narrative and a sense of identity to communities, and may well have been bound up with cosmogonies.

Human footprint tracks have been recorded at Goldcliff in the Severn Estuary and make the archaeological record wonderfully tangible (we can at least glimpse the Mesolithic sole, if not exactly their soul), but they also cause us to remember that these paths were lost and truncated during contemporary use. This will have impacted on the individuals' travel routes, and may have either removed or blocked access to traditional hunting grounds. Furthermore, if perceiving the landscape can be described as an act of remembrance,[3] how would a drastically changing landscape affect this? Are some

memories not regenerated when important cues in the landscape are lost? Who knows, but the loss of traditional paths is likely to have had considerable social implications.

The point here is that we have to think beyond inhabitants simply mapping their old places on to a new area, re-creating it elsewhere as land submerged. Place is far more complex than this. That is not to say that they could not re-create their cultural layout somewhere else, but rather that they could not merely transfer their embodied place, their memory place, their childhood place, the place that gave them and their community an identity. That, along with the narratives which kept those places alive, was lost during the process of the submergence of Northsealand.

As we saw in the previous chapter, human–environment relations are integrally linked. Modern Arctic groups may here provide a useful analogy to explore these relationships, and provide further ways of understanding the consequences of the changing environment for Mesolithic communities. In Sachs Harbour in Canada reports suggest that more frequent and intense storm events as a result of modern climate change are making boating conditions dangerous, as well as affecting the distribution of sea mammals.[4] Unpredictable storms can make travel and hunting difficult, and in Baker Lake in Nunavut, Canada, navigation has been affected, since winds are used for navigating the tundra. This is due to the fact that the prevailing northeast wind causes grass to bend and freeze in a southwest direction, allowing travellers to set their bearings, but unpredictable wind patterns mean that they now have to be careful when using these indicators for orientation.[5] The result of this is that there is a loss of trust in the weather and the landscape. Further, traditional hunting grounds are becoming inaccessible due to changes in the landscape, and some traditional campsites have been washed away by river surges caused by meltwater. Again, this is not just a practical problem, but constitutes an altered physical and psychological engagement with the inhabited world.

Inupiat communities around Barrow in northern Alaska have similar problems regarding whaling. As we discussed in Chapter 3, the Bowhead whale is central to their culture and each year there is an elaborate series of musical rituals involving singing, dancing and drumming, using drums made from whale skin. Through their skins the whales provide the music, enabling the mediation of human – whale relationships and closer ties to be constructed. Inconsistent wind directions, however, have made whaling difficult, with obvious economic implications for communities. More than this though: some believe that without a whale harvest there should not be any performances – as one community member put it, 'no whale, no music'.[6] This is partly the practical problem of a shortage of drum skins, but at a deeper level it shows that their relationship with whales has been fundamentally changed.

Whenever people are displaced, their world changes. In the 1950s the construction of the Kariba dam and subsequent widespread flooding of the Zambezi River in Africa resulted in the forced large-scale displacement of Gwembe Tonga tribes people from Zambia and Zimbabwe. Among the consequences of this was the loss of traditional shrines, which were not rebuilt due to the potential spiritual dangers emanating from the resettled area, including the existence of lingering ancestors. This had a profound impact on ritual activity, which was suspended for four years. Other recorded consequences included the movement away from kinsfolk creating a weakening of social ties, anxieties about new neighbours, and faith in many of the chiefs being eroded.[7] Similarly, resettlement of people from alongside the Volta River as a result of the Akosombo dam resulted in people sharing space with others 'whose languages and customs they did not understand', leading to anxiety.[8] Many of the gods of the Ewe and Akan people affected by the resettlement were linked to particular places in the drowned landscape, and while it was believed that some gods could be persuaded to move, others were so securely linked to places that they refused to leave and were inundated.[9] More recently, between 2005 and 2010, villages in El Gourna, Egypt were relocated from alongside the River Nile to a new site a few kilometres away in order to protect the historic environment. This led to significant social fragmentation, but one of the main consequences residents spoke of when later interviewed was the sense of loss and sadness experienced when leaving the old village. As one resident put it: 'painful, painful. My father and my mother they cried ... that was too sad. In old Gourna, it was my life and it was my memories.'[10] Relocation as a result of large development projects is, in modern times, the principal reason for human displacement, and there are few instances where resettlement has been able to improve, or even just maintain people's livelihoods.[11] While we obviously have to be careful in drawing comparisons from modern people, particularly agricultural groups, it is an understandable point that people are affected not just by losing land, but by losing their place and the personal meanings it holds.

These examples serve to show that changes to the landscape have major impacts on the environment and everything in it, including people. The effects are complex, involving a range of close interactions and cause-and-effect relationships, and the results are not always easy to predict as an outsider. People have a personal and intimate relationship with their surroundings, and when that environment becomes unfamiliar and its behaviour unpredictable and unexpected it creates a strong emotional response. The hunters in Nunavut, Canada, for example, who have had to change their hunting strategies and the locations of their campsites due to modern climate change, 'miss' the areas in which they use to hunt.

In some cases, these places have special significance to family heritage or hold meaningful memories for individuals. Many hunters and elders are extremely attached to the places they come from and travel to. They are tied to the land through their intimate knowledge of its paths and processes, but also through emotions and a sense of identity.[12]

This highlights the side to landscape change rarely discussed in the archaeological literature: such consequences do not come without considerable personal stress. That is to say, people are troubled by their land changing, and the forced changes to their lifestyle this entails, and it causes a degree of ontological stress. Hence, changes to the environment do not simply affect subsistence practices, but the individual and community's health and well-being, and people relate to the changing environment emotionally. Mental health problems such as anxiety, depression, stress, or even, in the case of sudden events, post-traumatic stress disorder, are acknowledged issues following flooding.[13]

It is also interesting to reflect on how those who moved from flooded regions were seen by others. As with modern traveller groups or refugees, being 'placeless' can also be a source of anxiety and a focus of suspicion from others, and it may have been so in the Mesolithic period. People without a place are frequently marginalized, homogenized and racialized; ethnic groups are often conflated into a single group identified by their very displacement: their placelessness. They become people 'out of place'; 'foreigners'. It is difficult to know how much this attitude is the product of a modern, sedentary view of the world; nonetheless, placeless people are likely to have been, at first at least, considered different – as 'other'. They would have had traces of elsewhere about them. This would have been particularly marked where one linguistic group moved into the region of another.

***

The Northsealand landscape, as with any other during the Mesolithic period, would have been named and would have retained social significance with stories attached to it. It is therefore not something that, as land was being submerged, could have easily been re-created elsewhere. It formed part of the fabric of people's being. When landscapes changed as a result of sea-level rise, both individuals' and communities' sense of being would have changed.

Mesolithic inhabitants of Northsealand must have had, at times, the sense of the ground shifting beneath their feet as the sea advanced and habitat disappeared. There would have been disorientation as the landscape was reshaped, becoming alien to the very people who had previously prided themselves on an intimate knowledge of it – this arcane knowledge of place rendered obsolete. Familiar geographies would have been disrupted and transformed, providing people with a sense of dislocation. When natural levees were overtopped and thresholds crossed, place was made strange and became defamiliarized, and as links with places were severed there must have been a form of disconnection. Places develop through an active engagement with the physical world; through the knowledge, the familiarity, the experience of it; the smell, the sound, the sight, the feeling, the pattern of the weather, the nature of the geology, flora and fauna. It is through all these factors that an understanding of place is formed, and by moving through this sensuous, embodied landscape, memories emanate and the world is opened up. Mesolithic inhabitants did not construct their world inside their heads, but engaged with it and dwelt in it. The loss of this landscape in the Mesolithic period – the loss of these places, these familiar locales where myths were created and identities formed – will have profoundly affected people's very sense of being.

Part Four

Responses

7

Living in a Changing World

Adapt or die goes the axiom. But adaptation is not a 'thing'; it is part of getting on with life. Adaptability or adaptive capacity is the ability to learn and adjust to changes in the environment, to moderate and mitigate possible damage, to take advantage of opportunities, and to cope with the consequences. We all do it to some extent.

Responses to change are difficult to categorize; however, different threads are apparent and over the next three chapters we will look at these. In particular they include the role of practice and belief, mobility and migration, knowledge and information (particularly how accumulated knowledge of the environment can increase resilience), social networks and exchange, flexibility, intensification, diversification, and technical adjustments. Let's not forget that opportunities can also come out of environmental change, such as experimentation, innovation and creativity, and these will be mentioned too. In practice, responses are likely to have been entangled and hybrid, combining many of these elements – which are, after all, fundamentally interrelated – rather than any single one.

One response to sea-level rise may have been to intensify ceremonial and ritual practice along the shoreline. The importance of the shoreline as a liminal and transitional zone from one spiritual domain to another has been highlighted in the archaeological literature,[1] and it may be that an advancing shoreline was of particular focus during periods of perceptible sea-level rise. This may be evident at a number of sites in The Netherlands, including at the Hoge Vaart-A27 site, where clusters of worked flint were buried, along with aurochs skulls, in wet and inundating locations.[2] Similarly, flint 'dumps' of axe knapping waste were recovered on a saturated shoreline at the Mesolithic settlement site of Vaenget Nord at Vedbaek, Denmark and there are marked concentrations of middle and later Mesolithic adzes and mace-heads along the shoreline in Norway.[3] The construction of the Europoort harbour near Rotterdam led to the discovery of over 500 bone and antler barbed points dating to the late Mesolithic period, and although these can be interpreted functionally, as, say, lost hunting gear, a ritual interpretation is far more intriguing.[4] Similar interpretations have also very tentatively been suggested for artefacts along the eroded Mesolithic shoreline beyond the settlement at Goldcliff in the Severn estuary.[5] It may be that artefact deposition occurred in land/sea transitional zones as it is precisely these areas where vegetation is sparse as a result of saltwater die-back and therefore the visibility of artefacts, however temporary, was most pronounced.[6] Later Mesolithic coastal middens around the North Sea basin frequently evidence formal deposition, such as axes, at Culverwell, Portland on the south coast of England,[7] or human remains, in, say, Oronsay, Scotland, Ferriter's Cove, County Kerry and Rockmarshall, County Louth in Ireland,[8] and perhaps reference 'some kind of textural boundary ... between land and sea'.[9] Mesolithic cemeteries also have a similar sea edge location, and some were clearly located on islands surrounded by water or on promontories, such as the cemeteries of Téviec and Hoëdic off the coast of Brittany, where they would have been rapidly cut off or covered. In some instances, the dead were even placed directly in or on the water, as can be seen in the boat burial at Mollegabet II in Denmark.[10]

One could envisage this as a way of placating the waters or water spirits that were transgressing onto land – a cry to the gods to make it stop; the buried flints a frantic offering to prevent the loss of stone sources in Northsealand. We could see the burials as further 'offerings' to the advancing shoreline, or the inundating landscape may have been utilized to keep the spirits suppressed and away from the living. This is much like the interpretation of figural sculptures at the Lepenski Vir site in the Iron Gates, Danube valley, which have been suggested as representing mythical ancestors ('fish-gods') intended to protect the settlements against the threat from flooding.[11] In this context, one can speculate as to the presence of a type of sea-level rise shamanism, similar to the Chumash Indian 'weather shaman' of south-central California.[12] Wetland deposition may therefore represent 'desperate shamanic attempts at maintaining social control and status' in the face of sea-level rise.[13]

Certainly sudden change, particularly a catastrophic event, has the potential to undermine confidence in religion, and may even facilitate the emergence of a new religious order. But we do not need to frame sea-level rise as an 'other' that needed pacifying; instead, it may be part of a broader process of mediation or negotiation with the landscape. As an alternative view, ritual deposition along the inundating shoreline could have been part of an ongoing process to fix people to that part of the landscape before it was lost. This may be particularly true of the coastal cemeteries, and perhaps we should see these burials as rooting people, or returning them to their ancestral land.

Evidence from Goldcliff suggests that the shoreline was used as a defecation zone in the Mesolithic period.[14] The rising sea level would, then, have removed this polluted space and therefore be seen as beneficial. Control of pollution plays an important role in the social life of modern groups,[15] and it is worth considering the function of rapid sea-level rise in this. In this view, votive depositions could be perceived as a way of ensuring *continued* sea-level rise and thus the permanent cleansing or mediation of the polluted zone. A similar case for the cleansing of a polluted land can be made for the siting of cemeteries in coastal locations.

Whichever way we choose to interpret these practices, the advancing sea was likely attributed with agency and identity. These practices may reflect the fact that the start of sea-level rise prompted a shift to a new relationship to this part of the landscape – a relationship that continued long after the Mesolithic period, and depositions in wetland areas are evident throughout later prehistory.

***

Mitigating the effects of rapid sea-level rise over a short time period would have included greater group mobility, and migration or relocation of people away from Northsealand's submerging land is the only real long-term solution.[16] Relocation is a common strategy among modern communities facing significant environmental change, again practiced at the individual and community level. Prehistoric hunter gatherers on the Kuril Islands in the Northwest Pacific adapted to tsunamis and intensive storm activity by moving settlements to high terraces and in more protected locations.[17] At Shapwick Heath in Somerset, a fundamental shift from the Mesolithic occupation of the lowland zone to upland areas is evident in the lithic and pollen record and linked to localized flooding.[18] Mesolithic Iron Gates settlements along the Danube valley were abandoned between 6300 and 6000 BC and may have relocated to higher terraces. This period corresponds with the '8.2 kya cold event', and therefore relocation could have been linked to extreme and unpredictable flooding events from the river.[19]

Migration, however, is not as straight forward as you might at first think. It is not simply an environmentally determined process and social aspects are of importance in shaping the decision to migrate from one's homeland. Holland Island in Chesapeake Bay, Maryland, USA, for example, was abandoned in 1920 following significant sea-level rise and loss of land. Neither loss of land nor changes to natural resources, however, were directly responsible for the abandonment, since the island remained habitable throughout the twentieth century. The island was abandoned due to loss of services, but more importantly, due to a general loss of faith in a future on Holland Island. After abandonment the attachment to the island remained, as people came crabbing in the summer for a number of years afterwards and reunions of former residents and their descendants still occur on the island.[20] This suggests that social issues may shape responses to sea-level rise more profoundly than the direct impacts of environmental change. The opposite is true of Funafuti Island, Tuvalu, in the South Pacific, where today people choose to remain on the island. This is despite knowing that it will be entirely submerged within decades due to its low elevation and rapidly rising sea levels (memorably described by the climate change writer Fred Pearce as 'toodle-oo to Tuvalu'). Factors influencing the decision to stay include a sense of identity and lifestyle provided by the island, as well as a strong faith that God will protect them.[21]

Although these examples clearly cannot be directly compared with prehistoric hunter gatherers, they do serve the purpose of showing people's wide, and sometimes contrasting, responses to sea-level rise. These two examples represent a bottom-up approach in the former with decisions made at the community level – the local scale – while the latter is an enforced, top-down decision, and this may explain the differing responses. But they do reveal that decisions on migration are frequently made on the basis of ontology as opposed to simple adaptive responses. In the area of the North Sea, islands permanently occupied by communities may well have been abandoned long before they became uninhabitable. A study of the southern Hebrides, for example, revealed an absence of settlement activity on the islands of Islay, Jura and Colonsay between 6050 and 5050 BC. This is a period that saw a rapid rise in sea level of the order of 6.5 metres over 100 years, and landscape changes would clearly have been evident over one or two generations. Although these islands remained habitable during this time, the period of abandonment (which coincides with the rapid rise) could be seen as a reflection of a loss of hope for the future of the island. As archaeologist Steve Mithen puts it, 'a Mesolithic forager may well have believed that the sea level was set on a course of continuous rise'.[22] Another group on a different island were just as likely to have responded entirely to the contrary.

Islanders will also have had ways of coping – for a while at least. People on Tikopia, a small island in the Solomon Islands, have coped with cyclones until recently by migrating temporarily to other islands and keeping their population low.[23] Strategies employed to enhance the latter included use of infanticide, abortion, marriage restrictions and allowing individuals to take suicide voyages out to sea.

There are no clues in the archaeology as to who had the authority to make decisions about when a community moved and to where, or who led migrations from submerging land, although it is an interesting point to consider. Following abandonment of a Northsealand island, communities may have returned temporarily by incorporating them into their subsistence strategies. This may have been to collect particular food sources, hunt seals, gather shellfish or to procure lithic raw material, as well as to maintain an ancestral attachment. Equally, groups may have clung onto a life on the island through a sense of place and identity long after it had become clear that it was being swallowed by the rising tide. Rising sea level throughout the Mesolithic period could have led to the continual movement of people further inland or to higher ground, or perhaps prompted widespread maritime dispersal.

***

Responses to environmental change are highly complex and very difficult to document, and there is no simple linear relationship between changes in the environment leading to a particular set of adaptations. Let us turn our attention now to ways in which people strengthen their resilience to environmental change.

8

Knowledge, Networks and Social Memory

Knowledge is empowering; there is no doubt about that. Perhaps, then, the single most important strategy for enhancing resilience to a changing environment is, quite simply, being informed. Having innate hazard awareness and a good knowledge base enables people to identify what is happening and to know how to respond. This is particularly important for responding to events or processes that may only become evident over extended periods, since it allows intergenerational communication. Through this it can also be honed from one generation to the next, ready to be implemented quickly during a period of rapid change. The availability of information about changes and risk clearly influences people's decisions and motivations for adaptive strategies. Knowledge is empowering – but it can also be restricted, controlled and traded more widely.

Encoding a variety of terms for recognizing changes to the landscape within language or art can be a way of precisely and accurately communicating information and observations, and may well have been used to pass on information of sea-level rise in the Mesolithic. Informal knowledge systems, such as storytelling, myth, folklore, ceremonies, music and artistic representations, provide a highly effective way of encoding environmental information and transferring knowledge of appropriate responses over long periods of time. This can include information about how to deal with, and what to expect from, the changing coastline, as well as ways of expressing human emotions to the loss of land; or even ways of keeping destructive, and perhaps tragic, events alive in people's minds. They can also act as a creative cue for thought about future decisions. In this way, experience of the realities of environmental change becomes built into social life and forms part of a worldview. This is demonstrated by the inhabitants of the Papua New Guinea Highlands who had a strong oral tradition of the AD 1660 Long Island volcanic eruption long after the event, while a number of Chinese myths, poems and songs relate to climatic fluctuations and flooding events, and are full of pragmatic advice.[1] It has also been suggested that Australian aboriginal art preserves memories of sea-level rise from long ago.[2] Encoded myths have often given societies knowledge for behaviour and thus saved lives; the Moken people of Thailand, for example, knew what to expect and what to do at the first sign of the tragic 2004 Indian Ocean tsunami (sail out to sea and meet the wave early) and as a result almost all survived.[3] This perhaps has some bearing on how we consider the impact of the Mesolithic Storegga Slide tsunami. Tareumiut and Nunamiut hunter fisher gatherers in Alaska encode information in their oral traditions. This includes knowing mythic tales which state that when sheep lack food they go to the sea and become beluga whales; and when beluga cannot find food they travel inland and become sheep; through these stories they know the practical advice that when beluga are scarce sheep are plentiful, and vice versa.[4]

Correspondingly, it has been suggested that some Palaeolithic art contained or embodied information about environmental change. Depictions of animals, their tracks and their habits (such as mating and defecation) may have been a way of broadcasting knowledge of the animals that informed hunting strategies.[5] In this way, it allowed others to cope better with the harsher conditions of the last glacial period and dwindling animal resources. Mesolithic mobile art may have similarly passed on abstract and symbolic information, and certain decorated artefacts with particular motifs in the Mesolithic may have represented 'a grammar of communication' and elements of 'information pathways'.[6] Lihult adzes have been suggested as carrying information about territorial cohesion across parts of southern Sweden, while similarly the shapes of the little flint micro- lithic points in the late Mesolithic of northwest Europe may have encoded information on territories.[7] Objects such as these may have been related to myths, allowing people to unlock information, such as about sea-level rise and past climates. If this all seems far-fetched, then think of the Mandé people of West Africa who use terracotta figurines to 'curate and transmit both past environmental states and possible responses to them'.[8]

In areas where disasters occur frequently, life may become regulated by taboos, well illustrated in Maori culture who established tapu over certain areas vulnerable to frequent volcanic activity in North Island.[9]

Ideologies often portray sudden environmental change as the result of some sort of social wrongdoing. Examples of this include the biblical story of Noah and the flood, or the AD 1607 tsunami or storm surge in the Bristol Channel and Severn Estuary, which was interpreted as God's warning to the people. The AD 1755 flood on All Saints Day in Lisbon was similarly framed as punishment for sin.[10] The Mandé of West Africa also see environmental crises as a consequence of malev- olent acts by people or spirits.[11] Others simply honour the event, such as the Mandan Indians in Missouri who hold an annual ceremony to commemorate 'the great flood'. This includes a representation of the first man, Nu-mohk-muck-a-nah, who relates the flood story. With an interesting link back to our discussion on ritual deposition, the final part of this ceremony involves collecting a pile of axes from the villagers and disposing of them in a deep part of a river.[12] Earthquake-induced tsunamis along the northwest coast of North America have been framed in myth as a battle between a great whale and a thunderbird.[13]

These narratives order both diachronic and synchronic events and give them reason, and such symbolism may include beginnings and ends or apocalypse and revival. Disaster ideologies often rotate in cyclical fashion, especially when environmental change is chronic, thereby making the unexpected expected; 'calamity does not imply loss, for all returns'.[14] By explaining environmental change in this way it becomes possible for people following social rules to come to terms with the changes. In some extreme circumstances too, it may encourage people to ignore the risks facing them. This may include culturally conservative groups that are unwilling to adapt to the changes facing them, such as the reluctance to abandon a shrinking island or to migrate from one area to another – an approach adopted by Tuvalu islanders.

Oral traditions are clearly an important way of passing information on – it is a sort of 'social memory'; the repository for captured experience and accumulated knowledge of change, and the arena in which ontologies of the world were formed, and adaptations formalized.

***

Adapting to sea-level rise and the associated land and resource loss could have been significantly enhanced by a detailed knowledge of the local environment. Indeed watching, understanding, interpreting and predicting the weather is a vital activity and an integral part of daily life in many modern societies, and the more precise one's observations are, the better the forecast. In the Arctic, watching the weather is a respected task, and people spend hours scanning the horizon and discussing indicators.[15] People, environment, birds, animals, plants, beliefs and weather are interrelated and in ceaseless motion with one another. Relationships are drawn between temperature fluctuations, wind strength and direction, wave energy, people's safety, animal behaviour, vegetation growth, and hunting success. People have a finely tuned awareness of these ever-changing relationships and learn to forecast the weather, read the terrain, judge the conditions, and predict animal movements and distributions. It is through many years of mentoring with respected experts that one learns to combine personal experience with generations of observed correlations between weather, land, sea and animals, and this in turn increases resilience to change. It helps people to construct knowledge of how to deal best with their changing environment. In this instance, knowledge of the weather is not simply handed down through generations as a cultural package, but is accumulated.[16] Part of this knowledge is phenology, the understanding of cyclic and seasonal phenomena: the knowledge of when flowers bud, fruits ripen, or when birds or animals migrate. Phenological data are about observation, experience and interpretation, and are based on long-term knowledge of a specific location.

Without drawing a direct parallel between the Mesolithic groups of Northsealand and Arctic communities today, it is likely that knowledge of the Mesolithic environment, and any changes to it, were accumulated through a similar experience of engagement; through continuous observations and daily encounters with the environment.[17] Through such deep phenological data, people could have developed a detailed knowledge and sensitivity to changes in the environment: an understanding of when thresholds were likely to be breached, the significance of dead woodlands, and the likely effect on resources and territory size. Appropriate responses could then have been formulated. These may have included avoiding areas vulnerable to flooding or collapsing cliffs, or knowing where the higher, safe areas are. They may also include making changes to subsistence patterns or adjustments to the timing of the seasonal calendar, modifying their hunting locations or exploiting a mix of species, and thereby minimizing risk and uncertainty.

By actively engaging with their surroundings and monitoring the environment, Mesolithic hunter fisher gatherers could build an accumulated knowledge of their changing environment that then increased their resilience to the changes taking place. By continually taking a measure of the changing (unfolding) landscape and of the situation, emotional responses are created. Emotional responses are important to the way people perceive, understand and interact with the world, and are motivated into action. Responses to environmental change are not simply economic efficiency, but are formed through a constellation of understandings, ontologies, perceptions and emotions.

***

Critical to effective information flow are vibrant social networks. Enhancing these can improve a group's ability to deal with change by offering access to resources unavailable locally, or improving understanding of the changes through information exchange. In the Mesolithic, the circulation of, say, beads as body adornments or stone raw material may represent part of a broader network of maintaining social relations during periods of rapid inundation. Indeed, almost all Mesolithic beads in Britain are connected with the sea or the shore, such as shells, beach shale or amber.

Mesolithic exchange networks in southern Scandinavia have been well studied, highlighting the role of figurines, pendants, star-shaped picks, and decorated bone and antler objects.[18] Exchange networks have been put forward as the reason for the distribution of Ertebølle shoe-last adzes in Sweden, as well as Lihult adzes across parts of southern Sweden, while Danish portable art has been suggested as providing evidence for exchange systems, and compared with the 'Kula Ring'. Certainly artefacts with certain dominant motifs, such as the 'wheatsheaf' design, are distributed widely across Jutland and Zealand and the archipelago of islands during the Mesolithic.[19] Within Britain, Portland Chert was clearly caught within such a network, found on Mesolithic sites from as far afield as Cornwall to the west and at sites such as Broomhill in Hampshire to the east.[20] The Severn estuary attests to contact of up to 100 kilometres, while Mesolithic lithics recovered from Priddy in Somerset may have derived from distances of forty kilometres.[21] There is also demonstrable movement and circulation of chert artefacts and raw material around the Peak District, Derbyshire in the late Mesolithic.[22] Clearly caught within exchange mechanisms, the value of these materials may have been as a medium for information exchange.

If one accepts that certain Mesolithic objects were part of an exchange system, they would have created alliances and obligations and established communication between groups, strengthening bonds. It could have structured marriage relations, so that exogamous interaction and the exchange of objects and information were part of the same network. In coastal areas, information exchange concerning sea-level rise may well have formed a part of these exchange networks. It certainly seems that the Chumash maritime hunter fisher gatherers in California developed strong social networks and alliances with groups from different environmental zones during the Medieval Climatic Anomaly, in order to share resources and therefore increase resilience to fluctuations.[23] As an interesting link with the British Mesolithic, they also increased production of shell beads during this period in order to exchange within these broader networks. Tareumiut and Nunamiut communities in northern Alaska frame food shortages as socially generated and requiring social mediation; this takes the form of an expansion of social networks, thus gaining access to a larger resource base.[24] Of course, social networks are easier to maintain when population densities are higher and settlements are closer together. This may mean that communities which lived on islands in Northsealand that were becoming increasingly cut off experienced social isolation, making it difficult to maintain such networks.

***

People learn about the environment and any changes to it as they develop, and from past events, and through this attunement can prepare themselves to cope better with future changes and events. By relying on a perpetual monitoring of the current situation, Mesolithic hunter gatherers were able to gain information on changes to the environment, however subtle. They could thereby make themselves resilient to, or even take advantage of, these changes as they arose. As we have seen, essential to this knowledge base were effective and advantageous social networks.

9

Being Pragmatic

Any sensible discussion of responses would be seriously lacking if it did not also include a few no-nonsense, practical answers to environmental change. The sort of matter-of-fact advice a sagacious parent might offer their adult child. So in this chapter I will explore a vignette of potential pragmatic responses to rapid change.

One such includes being flexible. In the Mesolithic this may have meant being able to move quickly to exploit any positive opportunities that arose, as well as to monitor ecosystems and resource stocks. The environment is constantly fluctuating, with an abundance of resources one year and scarcity the next; irregularity is a fundamental of the environment hunter gatherers live in, and responses to deal with fluctuations for resource procurement are a necessity of life. It is likely that Mesolithic communities lived within relatively fluid life ways, which would have been highly resilient to environmental changes. This is not to suggest that individuals were passively flowing with the environment, but that they were faced with a multitude of choices, which were adopted as appropriate to the individual circumstance.

Adapting practices specifically to sea-level rise may have included strategies such as locating freshwater sources away from inundating zones to avoid contamination from saltwater. It may also mean embracing an altered temporality, so that resources were used at different times of the year. Seasonally abundant plant foods may have been stored during periods of short-term fluctuations; acorns and hazelnuts, for example, are both easily storable and rich in calories, while fish can be smoked for later consumption. This is evident in the archaeological record, and a possible example of the latter may be detectable at Mount Sandal, Ireland, where posthole arrangements have been interpreted as fish drying or storage racks,[1] while pits filled with hazelnut shells in the southern Hebrides, Scotland may attest to storage pits, and large cylindrical pits have been interpreted as used for storage at the Mesolithic settlement of Auneau, France.[2] It is not unreasonable to assume that this was a familiar practice throughout the Mesolithic, and it has been suggested that storage was central to the late Mesolithic economy of the Iron Gates in the Danube valley, arguing that the stone-lined pits, usually interpreted as hearths, were used for storage. This latter example may have been a response to periods of cooling and flooding, such as the '8.2 kya cold event', which would have affected, among other things, fish migrations.[3] Other stored commodities could include prestige items for trade and exchange during lean years – another type of 'social storage'.[4] In this way, responses to the changing environment may have involved the intensification of certain resources, both economic and social.

Hand-in-hand with intensification is diversification – possibly because intensification leads to fluctuations in yields, requiring the exploitation of a greater range of species to make up the occasional shortfall.[5] There are certainly considerable benefits in diversifying resource and subsistence strategies, or by turning towards more readily available but perhaps less favoured foods. Various shifts in diet and subsistence strategies may be discernible across Europe in the Mesolithic,[6] and similar examples from around the North Sea basin no doubt exist. Intensification and diversification leave little archaeological trace, but it is interesting to consider what the archaeological record of such diversification would look like. Diversification as a way of responding to environmental changes can be seen in a very wide range of examples from across the globe and from different times. Animal bones recovered from archaeological sites in the area

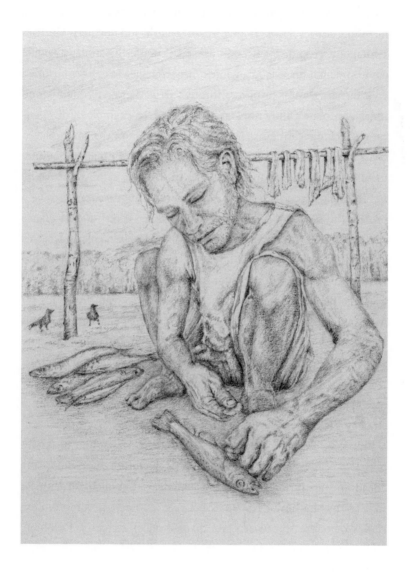

around Los Buchillones in the Caribbean evidence diversification of food resources from a range of environments and were interpreted as a resilient strategy against sudden disruptions to local environments, including sea-level rise.[7] In prehispanic central and northern Mexican settlements crop diversification was a risk-buffering strategy against environmental uncertainty, while other strategies may have included concentrating water resources through irrigation or terracing, food sharing, mobility and crop storage.[8] A modern example of diversification includes farmers in Maheshkhali upzali, on the southeastern coast of Bangladesh, who have turned from traditional agriculture to salt and shrimp farming to cope with heavy salinity intrusion. Interestingly here, farmers actively conserve mangrove forests to help protect the shoreline against coastal erosion.[9] While at first glance actively conserving an ecosystem in the Mesolithic period seems an unlikely response to sea-level rise, it is not impossible. There is growing evidence for a greater manipulation of the environment towards the later Mesolithic, including evidence from fish traps for woodland management such as coppicing and pollarding.[10] This is usually seen in terms of enhancing economic productivity (that is to say, improving the growth of particular forms of vegetation to attract wildlife as prey); however, it is worthwhile thinking of the possibility of active conservation being used in coastal zones as an adaptive strategy against sea-level rise.

Imposing restraints, quotas or even taboos on certain resources may also be a way of protecting them for the future. Indeed, looking ahead and nurturing resources in general is a resilient strategy, as well as the sharing of resources between and across communities; risk is therefore spread across a diverse set of activities. Flexibility and diversification again occur at the local level – that is to say, a bottom-up approach.

***

There were, no doubt, also technical responses to sea-level rise in the Mesolithic. To take an example of a rapid response – in areas prone to flooding people may have made adjustments to their dwellings to counter the incursion of floodwater or to prevent exposure and injury when floods enter. At Timmendorf-Nordmole I in the Wismar Bay, for example, a line of 'stepping stones' had been placed on waterlogged ground between the Ertebølle settlement and the shore.[11] Further afield, the Mesolithic buildings at Lepenski Vir, Padina and Vlasac along the Danube valley exhibit a number of rebuilds and internal reorganizations, possibly representing responses to damage caused during periods of extreme flooding as a result of climate change (namely the '8.2 kya cold event'). It has also been argued that the limestone floors at the site were a way of creating permanence in dwellings damaged by this postulated flooding of the Danube.[12]

In studies of modern communities living in the Mekong Delta in Vietnam, a number of household coping actions to flooding are evident, including avoidance of exposure to water in houses by raising furniture on bricks and creating raised walkways from planks, as well as the removal of unused vessels where mosquitoes can breed after flooding has receded.[13] The internal layout of houses in low-lying coastal areas could be adapted to militate against occasional flooding, by raising or suspending floors. Practical techniques may also have been used to warn of sudden floods; a traditional coping mechanism in northern Pakistan, for example, is to tie ropes with bells across rivers to provide warning of a flash-flood.[14]

As we have discussed, flint sources would have been cut off and submerged as a result of sea-level rise, impacting at a local level on what flint was used, the way it was used and the flint tools themselves. Indeed, tool changes have often been couched in terms of adaptations to the changing environment, usually suggested as a result of changes in the availability of game, although this rather assumes that environmental changes must have occurred in equal force across wide regions, impacting on everyone in the same way.

***

While the effects of sea-level rise would clearly have posed some challenges in the Mesolithic period, it would also have offered new opportunities, and sea-level rise does not have to be viewed as a negative in every respect. Experimentation, innovation and creativity would have increased the number of choices available to a group and are possible responses to the changing land, and this may include, for example, the adoption of farming.[15] Such an example illustrates how climate change may have provided opportunities for social, technological and economic change, although innovation should not be seen as necessarily the outcome of external factors alone.

A response to sea-level rise and the loss of land may have been to adapt to the seas in a far more intimate way. If, as suggested earlier, the coastal inhabitants of Northsealand were already closely identified with the sea, inundation of the area may have been positive. A perception of a widening sea may, therefore, have predominated rather than a loss of land. This sees the inundation from a maritime perspective, placing emphasis on the sea as somewhere to inhabit. A similar inversion of perspective may well have been created during the flooding of the Northsealand. The inundation of Northsealand may have encouraged people to take to the sea to visit traditional areas or make contact with distant relatives cut off as a result. People displaced by sea-level rise may not, therefore, have had to compete so much with other groups further inland, but instead spent more time at sea. In this way people may have identified with the sea, and become identified by their relationship with it. The loss of land in the early Holocene as a result of sea-level rise could, indeed, have led to some of the first seafaring groups in the British Isles.

***

Adaptation is a continual course of changes adopted to adjust life ways to a constantly changing world; it is an *ongoing process*, not a final state. People's perceptions and observations of environmental-change risks are the main determinants of adaptation.[16] That is to say that people operate in an environment as they see it, and it is through this perception that responses are developed. 'Perception guides action in accord with the environmental supports or impediments presented, and action in turn yields information for further guidance, resulting in a continuous perception–action cycle.'[17] This bottom-up approach focuses on the local-scale and particularly local-scale decision-making. Responses, by necessity, are local in scale, and people adapt, reorganize and adjust at an individual, household and community level.

There are different motivators and barriers that influence responses and these may include social norms and networks, gender, class or ethnicity. Differences would have occurred between communities, so that some communities would have been better placed to adapt than others. That is, they may have had greater access or entitlements to resources, better adapted to exploit terrestrial resources, or have advantageous social networks. Differences would have occurred within communities too; for example, some people would have been more skilful or more experienced than others and therefore likely to have taken advantage of certain situations more quickly. It is also worth noting that the environment affords some things but not others, and people are always tied to praxis and a particular historical environment where some things are possible but others are not. In this way, choices available were not unbounded. Nevertheless, a wide array of responses to sea-level rise could have been available to Mesolithic communities. Choices were available and local groups responded differently in deciding whether or not to change, move or maintain the status quo. Chosen responses were local or regional in scale, and decisions made at the individual, household or community level. This is the overwhelming evidence from studies of modern climate change; decisions are made by those directly engaging with the environment, with local knowledge of the environment and changes and traditional ways of coping with them.

Furthermore, emotional responses (feelings and passions such as joy, fear, honour, pride or a jealous rage) play a central role in understandings, motivations and bodily interactions with the world.[18] Emotions are primal driving forces that move people to action; they affect the way people engage, monitor and appraise the world around them; they emerge from interactions with the world and 'enter into our more conscious deliberations about how we should respond to our situation'.[19] Thus any response to sea-level rise is an emotional response as much as anything else. People do not always act wisely either, or with long-term futures in mind. Any account of past behaviour based on mechanistic judgement alone clearly misses a fundamental part of what it is to be human; the way people engage and interact with their surroundings.

The last three chapters have discussed a selection of possible responses based on a diversity of information, highlighting the complexity and multiplicity of choices available. Responses are conditioned by perceptions and understandings of the material world, and agency. They also comprise choice – the choice to do this over that, or to go here rather than there. These choices, made on the ground and based on knowledge acquired from the wider community, as well as personal experience of the environment, can vary according to changes in the environment, and perceptions of the environment.

Human behaviour is complex and rarely focused solely on expediency or resource needs; lives are rich with symbolism and loaded with social and ideological texture. We are not locked up in a world of our mind and it is not simply a process of computation in the head. Instead we make sense of the world through our situation in, and interaction with, the environment. As philosopher Alva Noë puts it, 'you are not your brain'; we are fundamentally embodied and involved with our environment; we are in it and of it.[20] Adaptations are not decisions imposed by environmental changes, and there is no simple cause and effect between them. Although a number of themes have been discussed, the reality would have been messy, entangled, interrelated hybrids of these, with many more that simply cannot be guessed at, and the consequences are just as likely to have been unintended as intended.

Part Five

To End

10

The Remembered Land

Humber, Thames: Variable 4, becoming 5 or 6 later. Rain and fog. Poor or very poor. Tyne, Dogger: Variable 4, becoming south or southeast 5 to 7, perhaps gale 8 later. Rain, fog patches. Moderate, occasionally very poor. Rockall, Malin, Hebrides: Southeasterly gale force 8 increasing to severe gale 10, veering south 5 to 7 later. Rain or squally showers. Good occasionally poor. Southeast Iceland: Northeasterly gale force 8, perhaps severe gale 9 later. Wintry showers, rain later. Good, becoming moderate or poor.

Standing on the Norfolk coast now and staring out across the North Sea at the seemingly endless expanse of water, the turbines on the horizon looking like toys placed by a playing child, it is easy to forget that this water overlies a once terrestrial landscape. Not just a land bridge that people journeyed across, but home to generations of people, a land of places and names and mythologies, and where lives were played out in all their exhilaration. It is also interesting to speculate how the encroaching seascape was understood and perceived by later communities. This final chapter outlines ways in which people in later prehistory and in the historic period perceived, engaged and responded to the new sea, and its power to give as well as to take.

***

Sea-level rise had slowed down considerably from the beginning of the Neolithic period; around the fourth millennium BC. Although there was a general background of rising sea levels, these fluctuated greatly with a series of rises and falls (transgressions and regressions). Land along the coastline continued to be inundated, and in the Fenlands in Britain a number of Neolithic sites, such as Shippea Hill and Hurst Fen, were affected by rising water levels.[1] The associated changing landscape in this area would have been both highly local and, at times and in places, rapid.[2] Fluctuations in sea levels have been observed in the East Kent fens continuing well into the late Holocene, and a Bronze Age barrow at Little Duke Farm, Deeping St Nicholas was submerged entirely.[3] The Blackwater and Crouch estuaries on the Essex coast also saw marine transgression in the later Neolithic period resulting in forest die-back.[4] In this way the coastline in later prehistory can be seen to have been very variable, with on the one hand land loss, but also the emergence of new land as a result of marine regressions. As with the Mesolithic period, this would have led, to some extent, to a social loss.

As sea levels rose in the Mesolithic period, higher areas were cut off and islands formed, some remaining evident across the new sea in the Neolithic period. The Cross Sands Anomaly and the higher chalk ridges around the Dover Straight, for example, would have remained above the water-line long after the low-lying areas had been drowned; although at the moment it is unknown when these areas were finally submerged. Other land masses that resolved into larger islands included the Frisian Islands, the Channel Islands, the Isle of Wight, the Isles of Scilly, and the Molène archipelago off the coast of Brittany. Islands such as these would have been homes to people, but they would also have provided convenient stopping points for seafaring communities. The newly formed North Sea was therefore a vector for mobility, with crafts crossing it and moving people, animals and objects such as axes. The area, though, would still have been undergoing considerable change, since the environment was one in which the effects of storms could have lasted much longer than elsewhere. This made for choppy waters and difficult tidal conditions, in which shallow subsurface features would have created shifting eddies, making for 'an unpredictable marine environment'.[5]

While the western seaways are often emphasized as an important route for Neolithic seafarers,[6] dredged artefacts remind us that the North Sea and English Channel were also travelled in the Neolithic period. These include two Michelsberg-style axes (dating to around 4200–3600 BC) dredged from around the Brown Bank area off The Netherlands coastline. As well as two small polished axes of volcanic tuff, possibly also dating to around 4000 BC, recovered from around the Dogger Bank area, a further axe has also been dredged from the Solent.[7] These axes, while possibly representing accidental losses – exports on their way to Britain and perhaps caught in a storm that overturned the boat – may equally represent an extension of the Mesolithic practice of formal deposition. In this way, the focus may have been the land below the waters on the seabed, leading us to ponder whether a social memory of Northsealand existed in the Neolithic world.

Similar activity may have occurred in the Bronze Age. Two collections of metalwork dating to between 1300 and 1150 BC have been recovered from offshore contexts around the British Isles: at Moor Sand, Salcombe in Devon, and Langdon Bay, Kent. These include weapons, tools and other bronze and gold artefacts and the former with a ploughshoe originally from Sicily.[8] Although these finds were not associated with boat remains or any other non-perishable items that might be indicative of being part of a cargo, they are frequently interpreted as the contents of a Bronze Age shipwreck.[9] Another way of interpreting these, however, is to see them as part of the broader Bronze Age depositional framework of placing metalwork in waterlogged areas; the sea representing the 'ultimate' wet place.[10]

By around 1000 BC the North Sea and English Channel had reached levels broadly comparable with today. As seen from the maritime activities of the Roman, Anglo-Saxon and Viking people, in the following millennia the sea became of fundamental importance in the movement of people, goods and for trade.[11] Increased mobility and advances in boat technology went hand in hand – mobility drove technology, which in turn created greater mobility. The growth in towns at this time fuelled a demand for fish, leading to greater use and exploration of the North Sea. Throughout this period the sea developed a distinct identity; different to land where there are trails and paths to follow; seafarers use the coastline and other features to form a 'nautical dwelling'. The sea was also an active agent in creating social identities for those using it and inhabiting the area around it.[12]

The coastal zone has always been dynamic; eroding cliffs, changing shorelines and removing land. A well-known example of this can be seen at the early medieval town of Dunwich in Suffolk, which was progressively lost due to cliff erosion. Dunwich was one of the principal medieval ports in Suffolk, and in AD 1086 had a mint, three churches and a population of over 200; by the thirteenth century it had at least eight churches. Following a storm in 1328, however, the harbour became choked with shingle and cliff erosion caused part of the town to collapse. Thereafter, and in the following centuries, the town was lost to the sea in sections.[13] Numerous other towns and villages have been lost in similar ways up and down the North Sea coastline, particularly along the Suffolk and Norfolk coast, while in Holderness alone more than thirty places mentioned in the Domesday Book have since been lost.[14]

Little is recorded of how people in the medieval period reacted to the destruction of their homes by the sea, but in subsequent generations losses such as these seize upon the imagination, as they are likely to always have done. Oral traditions around Dunwich claim that the sound of ringing bells can be heard coming from drowned churches beneath the sea in the advent of storms, perhaps attesting to the way people have dealt with the loss of place, particularly sacred sites, and as a way of keeping its memory alive. The sound of undersea bells is a persistent legend and known from a number of similarly lost sites, such as Aldeburgh, Felixstowe and Shipden off Cromer on the Norfolk coast.[15] Alternatively, legends can involve an act of divine vengeance, as in the case of Ravenser-Odd – a medieval town built on sand banks at the mouth of the Humber estuary. Ravenser-Odd was lost due to flooding, possibly a storm surge, in the fourteenth century, but according to the *Meaux Chronicle*:

Chiefly by wrong-doing on the sea, by its wicked works and piracies, it provoketh the wrath of God against itself. ... Wherefore ... the said town, by the inundations of the sea and of the Humber, was destroyed to its foundations.[16]

The 1607 storm surge or tsunami in the Bristol Channel mentioned in earlier chapters was similarly seen as God's warning. Others include the well-known legend of Lyonnesse (Isles of Scilly), while John Leland recorded an old myth of a lost land near St Michael's Mount off the coast of Cornwall. As maritime archaeologist Peter Murphy notes, 'the myths and legends of England incorporate what might perhaps be a folk memory of such losses'.[17]

The sea does not just take, of course; it also gives, and although the North Sea and English Channel remain active agents that still create identities, nowadays it is more often portrayed as a natural entity to be exploited. As well as fish and other seafood, this includes the extraction of gas, oil and marine aggregate deposits, the latter of which are used to supply the construction industry with nearly a quarter of its cement and concrete. Just as any disturbance of the ground on land can damage archaeological sites and deposits, so too can pipeline and cable laying or large-scale offshore developments, such as the exploitation of hydrocarbon reserves, the construction of wind farms or the expansion of ports. Damage is also caused by beam trawler fishing, as well as continued erosion by the sea. This growing economic exploitation of the North Sea and Channel seabed, though, has led to a greater exploration of submerged landscapes, as well as a greater need for legislation and management. In 2002 the National Heritage Act was passed in the UK, giving responsibility of the heritage within the English 12 nautical miles Territorial Limit to English Heritage (now Historic England). This thereby gave maritime sites parity with terrestrial ones, and extended the definition of 'ancient monuments' to include sites under the sea.[18] Coincident with this was the advent of the Marine Aggregates Levy Sustainability

Fund (MALSF) – a one-stage, non-deductible specific tax on the aggregates extraction industry. This allowed English Heritage to commission projects to improve knowledge of poorly understood landscapes that were at risk from aggregates extraction, including submerged landscapes, and minimize disturbance. Furthermore, in order to tackle issues surrounding the North Sea, including the commercial trade in trawled material by fishermen, a long-term, multidisciplinary project, known as the North Sea Project, involving a number of institutions and government organizations, as well as the cooperation of fishermen, was started in The Netherlands. The commercial trade is predominantly in Palaeolithic and Mesolithic bone and antler recovered from the dredged shipping lane known as the Eurogeul in the Southern Bight of the North Sea.[19] Collaboration between Rijksdienst voor het Cultureel Erfgoed, The Netherlands Natural History Museum and English Heritage has also led to the development of common archaeological frameworks.[20] Although the MALSF (and its terrestrial equivalent – ALSF) has now run its course, the legacy of projects funded through it is immeasurable, substantially contributing to our knowledge of submerged landscapes.[21]

Further developments have come from developer-led marine projects, particularly the push for sustainable energy and the associated construction of offshore wind farms. Archaeologists play an integral role within this industry, and archaeological mitigation, in one form or another, is commonplace. As a result, further evidence is becoming available and thus the potential for the recovery of *in-situ* material increases. Although sites are often small-scale with partial data coverage, and the areas targeted are not always of prime archaeological interest, these projects have nonetheless led to substantial improvements in our understanding of the potential of preserved offshore prehistoric landscapes, and there is now extensive evidence for near-shore Mesolithic palaeolandscapes around the coasts bordering the southern North Sea and English Channel. The number of offshore discoveries is ever increasing, while, as we saw in Chapter 1, 3D seismic data sets developed by the petroleum industry can be used to investigate the landscape below the seabed floor. These are exciting times for all of us.

***

This brings us back to the beginning of this book and the study of Northsealand over the last century. The archaeological study of sea-level rise can be traced from early recognitions of submerged landscapes in the nineteenth and early twentieth century through to mid- and late twentieth-century landscape reconstructions and discoveries; and from there to the more recent surveys that have revealed parts of this flooded landscape. These surveys have allowed a book such as this to be written. We can see Northsealand as an inhabited land – a place where entire lives were played out. The terrestrial sites give the now drowned area context, but the recognition is reciprocal, for it can now also provide these terrestrial sites with context. Detail of the character and dating of the landscape and a local-scale understanding of sea-level rise will, no doubt, lead in the future to more accurate descriptions of the effects of sea-level rise and how associated changes may have been perceived.

As we have seen, it is unlikely that Mesolithic communities perceived sea-level rise as a separate entity, but an integral part of their changing world. People were not just 'coping', but getting on with life – with all its trials and hardships, satisfactions and pleasures, and with a multitude of choices available. That is not to say, of course, that sea-level rise had no effect on people, for if one's environment changes, so too does one's experience.

Sea-level rise did not occur in isolation but alongside other environmental changes, and these would have created different challenges and opportunities. Climatic conditions during this period are likely

The Remembered Land 107

to have been highly variable with increased chances of changeable and unstable weather patterns.[22] Changes to the temperature and the environment would mean that some birds arrived and migrated at different times; for example, warmer temperatures would have led to wintering geese arriving later and leaving earlier, meaning fewer eggs were laid and reducing opportunities to hunt them. An analogy can be found in modern climate change in Britain, which is affecting the distribution and abundance of species, changing the timing of their reproductive events, and shifting distributions northwards and to higher elevations. The range margins of some creatures, such as butterflies, dragonflies and damselflies, are argued to be shifting at a rate of 12.5 to 24.8 kilometres per decade.[23] While this is proving beneficial for some species, it is severely affecting others, pushing them towards local extinction. Further, while year-on-year temperature rise is clearly affecting species, it is the increased extremes in weather that is having the greatest effect on British populations.

This would have been as true of the past as it is of today, and sudden environmental changes such as the drop in temperature as a result of the '8.2 kya cold event' will have had a huge impact. This would have led to, for example, the death of bird chicks and deer calves or affected the health and body condition of animals. While unusually hot weather would have caused larger animals to overheat, become exhausted and thin, leading to lower population levels. In Nain, Labrador, modern temperature rises are thought to be responsible for a greater number of sick and diseased animals, particularly parasites in the liver of caribou that affect the taste and texture of the meat.[24] Warmer weather in the Arctic has also increased the number of mosquitoes. These not only harass the caribou, influencing their health and distribution, but are also a nuisance to people, making travelling, hunting and camping more difficult.[25] It is reported that rising temperatures in the Canadian Arctic are affecting the caribou in ways that could not be identified in the archaeological record; for example, the meat now tastes different to the Inuit, and the skins are of poor quality.[26] This is probably the result of poor vegetation growth on which caribou feed, or changing vegetation, which then affect the health of the animals.

Periods of aridity would have affected some foods, such as berries, since a greater solar intensity would make berries smaller or shrivel, thereby reducing their value. Heavier rains are suggested by a shift to wetter conditions towards the end of the Mesolithic and could have affected, for example, bee populations and thus the pollination of fruiting species.[27] Changes in precipitation, particularly its frequency and timing, also affect soil conditions and river discharge, and consequently impact on the biodiversity of fish populations and certain macroinvertebrates.[28] Changes in the temperature would also alter river and lake levels,[29] which in turn affect the size of the fish. Warmer water temperatures may well increase the presence of parasites and the likelihood of infection by pathogens in fish. Fish metabolism is directly linked to water temperature, with direct consequences for food consumption, growth and foraging behaviour, and while higher temperatures can be beneficial for spawning, they can have fatal consequences for egg development.[30] Furthermore, water levels affect fish migrations upstream and into inland lakes, impacting on the location and timing of harvesting and therefore the local diet. Changes such as these, alongside changes associated with sea-level rise, could have had a profound influence on people's diets and resulted in considerable adjustments to their usual activities, to say nothing of the previously mentioned effect on ontological understanding.

This represents just a few selected examples of the ways in which climate change is profoundly impacting on people's lives today. Yet many of these impacts could not be identified from the archaeological record. Who could guess, for example, that warmer weather could affect the taste and texture of meat? Or that it would result in an increase in mosquitoes which then become such a nuisance that people even change their hunting habits, and animals their distribution? This emphasizes the challenges we face studying past climate change, and perceptions of past environments and the changes to them. Nevertheless, there is a need to better comprehend the array of human responses to environmental change and sea-level rise.

Nothing ever exists separately from its background – they are entangled with their contexts. In this way, Mesolithic communities would not have understood their environment as an external world of nature, with sea-level rise as something that had to be dealt with. They would have related to their surroundings just as they would with other humans, and these surroundings may include flora, fauna and physical entities such as the sea, all of which they were familiar with (and some of which may have had similar status to humans). This could have also included geophysical phenomena, such as sea-level rise and changing ecosystems. Think, for example, of the dog burials from Mesolithic cemeteries in southern Scandinavia mentioned earlier. Humans and dogs appear to have been treated in death in similar ways, in some instances receiving the same grave goods.[31] Their world was an integrated whole; the natural and cultural intertwined and interdigitated in all manner of ways.

It is not enough, therefore, to have an objective measurement of past sea-level rise; rather we need to understand the intersections between people and sea-level rise. In fact, the divide between society and nature is reflected in the very notion of measurable environmental change; that is to say, change that is separate from its cultural reading and interpretation. To elaborate slightly, climate change scientists monitor global climate through instruments (measuring things like temperature, rainfall and atmospheric pressure) in order to produce models of the changes taking place. However, these changes are frequently different to how the people living on the land (the local level) perceive their environment to have changed, and people are affected in ways that are not always obvious, or predictable, from the climate scientists' models. When scientists talk in the abstract of climate, the locals talk of weather: 'climate is recorded, weather experienced'.[32]

***

The approach taken in this book is an alternative to traditional conceptions of 'victims' of sea-level change; of legions of noble but head-bowed Mesolithic men, women and children, trudging away from their flooded homes. Instead, it is a holistic approach drawing the social, economic and environmental together. It has also highlighted the world as one of continuous change, transition and flux. The environment is not immutable, but constantly variable, forever changing and moving, eroding and depositing. This is particularly so with coastal areas, and especially during periods of rapid sea-level change. To those engaging with the coastal environment, change and dynamism are part and parcel of what it is. By actively engaging with the environment people were also immersed in the changes that took place; indeed the changes were an intimate part of their day-to-day lives, and people's relationship with the world was a dynamic one.

This book has stressed the close and intense relationship between humans and their environment, and sea-level and climate change can, and should, act as a touchstone for how we think about those relations. To fully understand the effects of sea-level rise, a non-dualistic view of the body and the environment as one process is needed. Through this, a fresh approach to understanding past environment changes and a richer and more complex story of sea-level rise and the Mesolithic period can be developed. The sea connects Britain with Europe, and Northsealand connects us all to the past.

Epilogue

The two brothers huddled together, their bodies pulled tight into cloaks sodden with rain and spray from the sea. The boat growled with every wave; rhythmically rocking the men as it mounted each rolling upswell, cresting in time for the next. As far as the eye could observe was sea, and it had been so long since leaving the last island that the sun, glimpsed only occasionally through dark mackerel clouds, had spanned the sky. This landscape is barren to the terrestrials, to the farmers who know not of the wetlands and the mighty gorge below, but to these men it is replete with meaning. They spent their lives at sea – their mother used to say they had been born in a boat – and for them the rich texture of the watery surface is as readable as the land, full of named locales reflecting its form and character. They know where to find the shoals of fish, the oyster beds and seal pups. They know the dangerous places never to cross, and they know of the ground beneath, the rises and falls that were once rolling hills and river valleys, and where, at low tide in shallows around islands, to see dead trees protruding from the water like the grisly teeth of a wretched monster. And they know, through stories told and retold to them by their parents, that this was the drowned land of their ancestors.

Ahead they could see something – a subtle change in the timing and direction of the undulations; white caps now just visible on the wave peaks reflecting a slight rise in the seabed below. They had arrived. They had told stories of their childhood all journey, but barely a word had been uttered since leaving the last island, and now the silence seemed to deepen. Bending, a brother pulled out a large object from under his seat and laid it on his lap; the cloth wrapping falls open at one end revealing the glossy red surface of two polished axes lying one on top of the other. The other watched quietly, fingering a leathery pouch beneath his cloak – the burnt bones unmistakable within. The movement of the boat changed as they entered their destination, and simultaneously they slid across to one side, pausing briefly to look at each other before tenderly holding out their arms and allowing the offerings to drop through the water to the land below. Their mother had finally returned to her ancestral homeland. Like droplets of water emerging from a spring and setting on a journey across land, it all ends with the sea.

***

Two brothers work at the side of a boat; one operates the winch while the other guides the net up as it emerges from the water with a roar. The net swings across and with a yank from the younger of the two, its fishy contents spill onto the deck. 'There are bones in this one', he says, 'what shall I do?' 'Throw them back in', replies his brother walking away, before pausing and turning, 'keep the mammoth tooth though – we can sell it on eBay.'

Meanwhile, in a different part of the world, a man stands in the shallow sea, his trousers rolled up to his knees. A camera, set on the beach, watches him as he talks about his family and his land. And he tells the world that this land, under the water, was once his family's home.

Notes

Recognizing Northsealand

1   The 'Ice Age' referred to here and in the subtitle of the book is used colloquially and really refers to the last glaciation; we are still actually within the Ice Age, and so in that sense it has not ended.

2   The name 'Doggerland' was first coined by Bryony Coles in 1998 in honour of Clement Reid's suggestion that the area was once dominated by the 'Dogger hills' (now the Dogger Bank). Vere Gordon Childe, however, had already referred to the area as 'Northsealand' in his later books (the sixth edition of *The Dawn of European Civilization*, 1957: 37, 47; and *The Prehistory of European Society*, 1958: 27–30) (see also Saville 2009). Most authors now refer to it as Doggerland, although some use Northsealand or North Sea land (such as Strassburg 2000: 95; Momber et al. 2011: 160). Recent work has shown that the Dogger Bank (as with other sandbanks) is largely the result of recent submarine deposition and, therefore, would not necessarily have been an obvious topographical feature during the early Holocene (Gaffney et al. 2009: 68; Peeters et al. 2009). This, to my mind at least, rather undermines the name Doggerland. Although Doggerland does have an appeal, and has certainly become firmly ensconced in the public's collective mind, in this book Northsealand has been favoured, or, occasionally, the North Sea plain or lowlands. The English Channel area is included within this name.

3   Giraldus Cambrensis (1191: 1908 edn).

4   Coles (1998); Bell (2007).

5   Reid (1913: 9).

6   Lubbock (1913: fig. 255).

7   Fletcher and Kipling (1911: 9).

8   For example, Godwin (1943).

9   Burkitt (1932).

10   Clark (1936: 86–7); Clark and Rankine (1939: 98). Also see Clark (1975: 28).

11   Coles (1998: 50).

12   Reid (1913: 3).

13   Coles (1998, 1999, 2000, 2013) for a retrospective.

14   Childe (1942: 50–1); Wheeler (1954: 231).

15   There are many new and innovative studies of the Mesolithic period available – see, for example, Conneller (2004); and papers in Conneller (2000); Conneller and Warren (2006); Milner and Woodman (2005); Bevan and Moore (2003). For the literature on the prehistory under the North Sea, see papers in Flemming (2004); Rensink and Peeters (2006); Waddington and Pedersen (2007); Gaffney et al. (2007, 2009); Peeters et al. (2009); Benjamin et al. (2011); Van de Noort (2011).

16   For example, Jelgersma (1961, 1979); Lambeck (1995); Coles (1998); Shennan and Andrews (2000).

17   Shennan and Andrews (2000); Shennan and Horton (2002).

18   Fitch et al. (2005); Gaffney et al. (2007). See Gaffney et al. (2009) for a good description of seismic survey, and the processes involved in making the data 3D. See also Gupta et al. (2004, 2007).

19   Such as Ward et al. (2006); Behre (2007).

Thinking the Imagined Land

1   I have attempted here to integrate information from both UK waters and those belonging to continental countries, although the information is heavily skewed towards the area within twelve nautical miles of the British coast. This is largely due to the impressive amount of work funded by the Marine Aggregate Levy Sustainability Fund (MALSF) (now sadly defunct). At this stage, comparable evidence simply barely exists from the continental side (with the Rhine/Meuse area being a notable exception).

2   Simmons et al. (1981); Bell and Walker (2005); Huntley and Birks (1983).

3   Cameron et al. (1992); Fitch (2011); Tappin et al. (2011).

4   This area has been studied in detail and characterized by the MALSF-
    funded North Sea Palaeolandscapes Project (NSPP) conducted by the
    University of Birmingham (Gaffney et al. 2007, 2009; Fitch 2011), and
    this description is taken from their work.

5   Clark (1954); Conneller and Schadla-Hall (2003); Conneller et al.
    (2012); Dark et al. (2006).

6   Gaffney et al. (2007). This valley was also investigated as part of the
    Humber Regional Environmental Characterisation report (REC) and
    the information here also comes from Gearey et al. (planned for 2015).

7   Holford et al. (2007); Fitch et al. (2007: 107).

8   Sainty (1924).

9   For example, Tappin et al. (2011: 98) suggest Sand Hole and Silver Pit
    would have drained the Humber and Wash respectively. Markham's
    Hole is also likely to have been a freshwater lake during the early
    Holocene. See also Dix and Sturt (2011: 9).

10 Limpenny et al. (2011).

11 Murphy (2007: 10).

12 For example, Conneller (2006).

13 See Bradley (2000) for a discussion of Ukonsaari.

14 For example, Hardy and Wickham-Jones (2009); Chatterton (2006).

15 Tappin et al. (2011: 101–2). The seismic survey data for the North Sea
    Palaeolandscapes Project (Gaffney et al. 2009: 68) have also revealed
    an early Holocene landscape underlying the Dogger Bank, which again
    suggests that these banks formed after the landscape had submerged.

16 For the latter point see Peeters et al. (2009: 24).

17 Limpenny et al. (2011: 258). See Hijma and Cohen (2011) for the
    continental side.

18 After Hijma and Cohen (2011). The gorge had formed in the Weald-
    Artois chalk ridge during an earlier interglacial period: Gupta et al.
    (2007).

19 Rankine (1936, 1948, 1949a, 1949b); Clark and Rankine (1939: 95–6);
    Jacobi (1978); Reynier (2005).

20 James et al. (2010); Arnott et al. (2011).

21 For example, Green (2000: 27–8).

22 Information from the MALSF-funded Seabed Prehistory project: Wessex Archaeology (2008a, 2008b, 2008c).

23 James et al. (2010, 2011).

The People of Northsealand

1 Glimerveen et al. (2004); Kolfschoten and Essen (2004).

2 Andersen (1985, 2011); Fischer (2004); Grøn and Skaarup (2004a, 2004b); Uldum (2011); Rieck (2003).

3 These sites include Jäckelberg-NNW, Jäckelberg-Huk, Jäckelrund-Orth, Jäckelberg-Nord and Timmendorf-Nordmole: Lübke et al. (2011); Lübke (2003).

4 Verhart (2004).

5 Louwe Kooijmans (2003).

6 The information here comes largely from excavations at the sites of Schokland-P14, Emmeloord-J97, Urk-E4 and Hoge Vaart-A27; Peeters (2006, 2007); Maarleveld and Peeters (2004).

7 Crombé (2006); Crombé et al. (2011).

8 Within the Solent Basin see Field (2008: ch. 3). For work on the Isle of Portland see Palmer (1977, 1989). For Hengistbury Head see Barton (1992). For Mesolithic flint scatters in Hampshire see Bradley and Hooper (1975); Draper (1968); and in Sussex see Pitts (1980); Jacobi (1978); Palmer (1977); Wymer (1977). For the Somme and Picardy area see Ducrocq (2001); Ducrocq et al. (2008). For the Seine and Haute-Normandie see Souffi (2004, 2008). For north Cotentin see Ghesquière et al. (2000). And for Brittany see Marchand (2005, 2007). Also see Ghesquière and Marchand (2010); Conneller et al. (planned for 2015).

9 Momber (2004); Momber et al. (2011).

10 Allen and Gardiner (2000).

11 For more on this, see Conneller (2006); Chatterton (2006); Milner (2006).

12 Spikins (1999); Rowley-Conwy and Zvelebil (1989). For fish traps see Fischer (2004); McQuade and O'Donnell (2007, 2009).

13 From Aggersund and the late Mesolithic site of Sølager (Rowley-Conwy and Zvelebil 1989), the latter of which also included bones of eider and velvet scoter.

14 Rowley-Conwy and Zvelebil (1989).

15 Smith (1992); Spikins (1999); Bang-Andersen (2003); Fitch (2011).

16 Sakakibara (2009).

17 Evidenced at Howick, Northumberland (Waddington 2007), Oronsay (Mellars 1987) and Scandinavia (Kvamme and Jochim 1989). In fact, some sites of this date in the Baltic regions are dominated by seal bones; Rowley-Conwy and Zvelebil (1989). See Clark (1946: 12) for more on the Mesolithic exploitation of seals.

18 Clark (1954).

19 Harris (2013); Pollard (1996).

20 Jones (2010).

Shaping the World with Ice and Sea

1 This description comes from Clark et al. (2012).

2 Johnson et al. (1993); Clark et al. (2012).

3 Fairbanks (1989); Lambeck et al. (2010).

4 Church et al. (2010a).

5 Mitrovica et al. (2010); Shennan (1989); Shennan et al. (2012).

6 Kiden et al. (2002) have provided evidence from both model and observational data for a forebulge under the North Sea. This was centred on Northsealand between Norway and Britain and extended through northwest Netherlands and northern Germany. These observations are backed up by the work by Vink et al. (2007), which indicates that the area which is now the southern North Sea subsided relative to Belgium between 8050 and 2850 BC probably as a result of forebulge collapse.

7 Johnston (1995).

8 Church et al. (2010b).

9 Sturges and Hong (2001).

10 Fairbridge (1983).

11   This modelling ranges from Lambeck's 1995 geophysical model (GB-3) aimed to predict ice retreat across Great Britain to Peltier's model (ICE-1), which has been subsequently modified (ICE-2, ICE-3G, ICE-4G) and its parameters constantly refined; Peltier (1994), 1998, 2002); Shennan et al. (2000, 2006). For General Circulation Models see Horton et al. (2008); PALSEA (2010).

12   Steffen et al. (2010); Hansen (2005); Zwally et al. (2002); Joughin et al. (2004).

13   See Tooley (1978, 1985); Mörner (1976a, 1976b); Kearney (2001) for the difference between smooth and oscillating sea-level curves. Also Shennan (1987).

14   Known as MWP-1A. Huang and Tian (2008); Eren (2012).

15   Known as MWP-1B. Huang and Tian (2008).

16   Huang and Tian (2008); Bird et al. (2007).

17   Thomas et al. (2007); Garnett et al. (2004).

18   Barber et al. (1997); Clarke et al. (2004); Hijma and Cohen (2010).

19   Known as MWP-2. Blanchon and Shaw (1995); Bird et al. (2007); Lambeck et al. (2010); Yu et al. (2007).

20   Blanchon and Shaw (1995: 4).

21   The suggestion that there was a major tsunami generated by an underwater slide off the coast of Norway during the Mesolithic period was first made by Svendsen, when deposits were identified along the Norwegian coast (Weninger et al. 2008). Corresponding deposits have since been identified in eastern Scotland (Dawson et al. 1990; Long et al. 1989; Smith et al. 1985, 2004), as well as in a number of other regions around the North Atlantic, seemingly reaching as far as the east coast of Greenland (Wagner et al. 2007).

22   Bondevik et al. (2005); Weninger et al. (2008); Smith et al. (2004); Wagner et al. (2007); Boomer et al. (2007). For the time of year of the tsunami see Rydgren and Bondevik (2015).

23   Weninger et al. (2008: 16).

Changing Worlds

1 Nicholls and Leatherman (1995); Nicholls (2010).

2 Leatherman (2001).

3 Kearney and Stevenson (1991); Leatherman (2001).

4 Hijma and Cohen (2011).

5 Keith (2010).

6 For information on broader vegetation changes throughout the Mesolithic period see Spikins (1999); Macklin et al. (2000); Tipping (2004); Tipping and Tisdall (2004); Tipping et al. (2008).

7 Harris (2000: 56).

8 Leatherman (2001); Bruun (1962).

9 Douglas (2001: 2); Leatherman (2001); Nicholls (2010).

10 Nicholls et al. (2007).

11 McMichael et al. (2006); Haines et al. (2006); Few et al. (2004a); Costello et al. (2009); Patz et al. (2005).

12 Few et al. (2004a).

13 See Sallares (2006) for more on the role of sea-level rise in the spread of malaria throughout the Holocene.

14 Lowe et al. (2010).

15 McRobie et al. (2005); Bryant and Haslett (2002); Haslett and Bryant (2004).

16 Lowe et al. (2010).

17 Thibault and Brown (2008).

18 See Tipping and Tisdall (2004).

19 Chu (2007).

20 Rowley-Conwy (1981, 1984). Although more recent work at other midden sites, such as Norsminde in Denmark, suggest a continuity of oyster exploitation into the Neolithic period; Milner and Laurie (2009).

21 Austin (1991); Shennan et al. (2000). Possible evidence for the consequences of this comes from the Rhine/Meuse flood basin where it is thought to have caused the rapid abandonment of some channels, such as the Meuse (Hijma and Cohen 2011). Long et al. (1996) have also identified sediments on the southeast coast of England indicative

of chaotic tides, which they suggest might be associated with this breach.

22 Milner and Laurie (2009).

23 Nicholls et al. (2007).

24 Sievers (2012).

25 As suggested by Waddington (2007: 197).

26 Johnson (2000).

27 For evidence of violence at Skateholm see Larsson (1988a; Mithen (2003); and beyond see Price (1985); Schulting (1998); Thorpe (2003).

28 Conneller et al. (2012); Conneller and Schadla-Hall (2003).

29 Pitts and Jacobi (1979).

30 Crombé et al. (2011: 468).

31 Akter (2010).

32 Gbetibouo (2009).

Losing Place

1 Basso (1996: 134). For other examples see Rumsey (1994); Smith (1999); Morphy (1991).

2 Kelly (2003); Broadbent and Edvinger (2011); Bradley (2000); Papers in Jordan (2011); Brody (2001: 35).

3 As described by Ingold (2000: 189).

4 Jolly et al. (2002).

5 Fox (2002).

6 Sakakibara (2009).

7 Torry (1978).

8 Torry (1978: 175).

9 Yarrow (2011).

10 Duggan (2012: 20).

11 Scudder and Habbob (2008).

12 Fox (2002: 44).

13 Few et al. (2004a).

Living in a Changing World

1　For example, Bradley (2000); Pollard (1996); Menotti (2012: 188–202); Brown (2003).

2　Peeters (2007: 201–2).

3　Petersen (1989: 328) for the former, Bergsvik (2009) for the latter.

4　Verhart (2004).

5　Bell (2007: 225).

6　Evans (2003).

7　Palmer (1999).

8　Conneller (2006); Chatterton (2006).

9　Evans (2003: 61).

10　See Mithen (1994: 120); Zvelebil (1986: 172) for comments on their coastal locations; Larsson (2003); Zvelebil (2003: 7, 10) for comments on burials in water; for the Danish boat burial see Grøn and Skaarup (1991, 2004a, 2004b); and for Téviec and Hoëdic see Schulting (1996).

11　Bonsall et al. (2002a).

12　Johnson (2000).

13　Strassburg (2000: 115).

14　Bell (2007).

15　See Douglas (1966) for a classic account of pollution.

16　For example, Jacobi (1979); Binford (1968); Price (1987). See Schmitt et al. (2006); Johansson (2003) for comments on migration and the colonization of parts of Scandinavia; and Passmore and Waddington (2012) for a discussion of the movement of displaced groups around Britain.

17　Fitzhugh (2012).

18　Bond (2009).

19　Bonsall et al. (2002a); Bonsall (2008: 265).

20　Arenstam Gibbons and Nicholls (2006).

21　Mortreux and Barnett (2009); Pearce (2007: 55).

22　Mithen (2000: 622).

23　Torry (1978).

Knowledge, Networks and Social Memory

1   Gratton (2006); Hsu (2000).

2   Flood (1983: 143).

3   Krajick (2005).

4   Minc and Smith (1989).

5   Mithen (1990).

6   Zvelebil (2011: 197).

7   Bengtsson (2003) for the former point and Gendel (1984) for the
     latter.

8   McIntosh et al. (2000: 24).

9   Gratton (2006: 15).

10   Bell and Walker (2005: 173).

11   Togola (2000: 187). See also Echo-Hawk (2000).

12   Matthiessen (1989: 152–4).

13   Krajick (2005).

14   Hoffman (2002: 134).

15   Krupnik (2002).

16   Ingold and Kurtilla (2000: 187).

17   The same point has been made by Steve Mithen, who points out that
     Mesolithic period sites in the southern Hebrides are mostly located
     with good views across the land (Mithen 2000: 605).

18   See Larsson (1988b, 1990a); Strassburg (2000); Zvelebil (2011).

19   Mesolithic period exchange has been widely discussed. For shoe-last
     adzes see Edenmo (2009). For Lihult adzes see Bengtsson (2003). For
     Danish portable art see Nash (1993). With regard to the circum-Baltic
     region more broadly see Zvelebil (2006, 2011). For central Europe
     see Kind (2006), and for southeast Europe see Voytek and Tringham
     (1989).

20   Chatterton (2006).

21   Bell (2007) for the former and Taylor (2001) the latter.

22   Hind (2004).

23   Johnson (2000).

24   Minc and Smith (1989).

Being Pragmatic

1   Woodman (1985).
2   Mithen (2000) for the former and Verjux (2003) for the latter.
3   Voytek and Tringham (1989); Bonsall (2008).
4   Rowley-Conwy and Zvelebil (1989).
5   Mithen (1990: 247).
6   Just to take a few examples, off the Baltic coast Ertebølle settlement evidence suggests a shift from terrestrial resources and freshwater fish to progressively greater exploitation of marine resources (Lübke 2009; Zvelebil 1989); elsewhere, a shift in subsistence strategies towards a broad spectrum of resources during a period of rapid environmental change in the Mesolithic has been suggested, for example, at Grotto del'Uzzo in northwest Sicily (Mannino and Thomas 2009) or in the Italian Alps (Grimaldi and Flor 2009).
7   Cooper (2012).
8   Nelson et al. (2012).
9   Akter (2010).
10 For example, Simmons (1996). For fish traps see McQuade and O'Donnell (2009); Pedersen et al. (1997).
11 Lübke (2009: 560).
12 Radovanović (1996: ch. 3); Bonsall et al. (2002a); Bonsall (2008); Borić and Miracle (2004).
13 Few et al. (2004b).
14 Davis and Hall (1999).
15 Bonsall et al. (2002b); Tipping and Tisdall (2004); Turney and Brown (2007).
16 Grothman and Patt (2005).
17 Gibson and Pick (2000: 16).
18 For more on this see Damasio (1999, 2003, 2012); Johnson (2007); also Mithen (1991); Gosden (2004) for a discussion of this within the archaeological sphere.
19 Johnson (2007: 61); Damasio (2003).
20 Noë (2009: 142).

The Remembered Land

1   Clark and Godwin (1962); Smith et al. (1989); Clark (1960).

2   Sturt (2006).

3   Long (1992); Van de Noort (2011).

4   Murphy (2007, 2009).

5   Garrow and Sturt (2011: 63); Callaghan and Scarre (2009).

6   Case (1969); Callaghan and Scarre (2009); Garrow and Sturt (2011).

7   Van de Noort (2011); Murphy (2009).

8   Needham and Giardino (2008).

9   For example, Murphy (2009).

10 Samson (2006: 380).

11 Osler (2007); Murphy (2009).

12 Van de Noort (2011).

13 Murphy (2009); Parker (1980).

14 Allison (1955).

15 Westwood and Simpson (2005); Murphy (2009: 179) for further sites.

16 Quoted in Westwood and Simpson (2005: 383).

17 Murphy (2009: 177).

18 Roberts and Trow (2002); Flemming (2002); Oxley (2004).

19 Glimerveen et al. (2004); Mol et al. (2006).

20 For example, Peeters et al. (2009).

21 These projects include, among many others, the University of Birmingham's North Sea Palaeolandscapes Project, Wessex Archaeology's Seabed Prehistory and Palaeo-Arun projects, and four regional marine characterizations. Respectively: Fitch et al. (2005); Gaffney et al. (2007, 2009); Wessex Archaeology (2007, 2008a, 2008b, 2008c); Tappin et al. (2011); Limpenny et al. (2011); Dix and Sturt (2011); James et al. (2011).

22 See, for example, Anderson (1998); Anderson et al. (1998); Macklin et al. (2000); Magny (2004); Mayewski et al. (2004).

23 Hickling (2006: 136).

24 Furgal et al. (2002).

25 Thorpe et al. (2002: 214).

26 Fox (2002).

27 Anderson (1998); Tipping (2004); Tipping and Tisdall (2004); Tipping et al. (2008).

28 Sievers (2012).

29 As evidenced in the archaeological record: Digerfeldt (1988); Sarmaja-Korjonen (2001); Macklin and Lewin (2003); Magny (2004).

30 Sievers (2012).

31 Larsson (1990b); Bradley (1997, 2004).

32 Ingold and Kurtilla (2000: 187). And see papers in Krupnik and Jolly (2002).

References

Akter, A. *Household Level Vulnerability to Sea-level Rise in Bangladesh. Risks, Perceptions and Adaptation in the Coastal Areas.* Saarbrücken: Lambert Academic Publishing, 2010.

Allen, M. J. and J. Gardiner. *Our Changing Coast: A Survey of the Intertidal Archaeology of Langstone Harbour, Hampshire.* York: Council for British Archaeology (CBA Research Report 124), 2000.

Allison, K. 'The Lost Villages of Norfolk', *Norfolk Archaeology* 31 (1) (1955): 116–62.

Andersen, S. H. 'Tybrind Vig, a Preliminary Report on a Submerged Ertebølle Settlement on the West Coast of Fyn', *Journal of Danish Archaeology* 4 (1985): 52–69.

Andersen, S. H. 'Ertebølle Canoes and Paddles from the Submerged Habitation Site of Tybrind Vig, Denmark', in J. Benjamin, C. Bonsall, C. Pickard and A. Fischer (eds), *Submerged Prehistory*, 1–14. Oxford: Oxbow Books, 2011.

Anderson, D. E. 'A Reconstruction of Holocene Climatic Changes from Peat Bogs in North-west Scotland', *Boreas* 27 (1998): 208–24.

Anderson, D. E., H. A. Binney and M. A. Smith. 'Evidence for Abrupt Climatic Change in Northern Scotland Between 3900 and 3500 Calendar Years BP', *The Holocene* 8 (1998): 97–103.

Arenstam Gibbons, S. and R. Nicholls. 'Island Abandonment and Sea-level Rise: An Historical Analog from the Chesapeake Bay, USA', *Global Environmental Change* 16 (2006): 40–7.

Arnott, S. H. L., M. Leivers, D. Pascoe, S. Davidson and P. A. Baggaley. *EECMHM Archaeological Characterisation. Use Many Times: Archaeological Interpretation of Eastern English Channel Datasets.* Wessex Archaeology Report 72640, 2011.

Austin, R. M. 'Modelling Holocene Tides on the NW European Continental Shelf', *Terra Nova* 3(1991): 276–88.

Bang-Andersen, S. 'South-west Norway at the Pleistocene/Holocene Transition: Landscape Development, Colonization, Site Types,

Settlement Patterns', *Norwegian Archaeological Review* 36 (1) (2003): 5–25.

Barber, D. C., A. Dyke, C. Hillaire-Marcel, A. E. Jennings, J. T. Andrews, M. W. Kerwin, G. Bilodeau, R. McNeely, J. Southon, M. D. Morehead and J. M. Gagnon. 'Forcing of the Cold Event of 8,200 years ago by Catastrophic Drainage of Laurentide Lakes', *Nature* 400 (1997): 344–8.

Barton, R. N. E. *Hengistbury Head Dorset. Volume 2: The Late Upper Palaeolithic and Early Mesolithic Sites*. Oxford: Oxford University Committee for Archaeology (Monograph No. 34), 1992.

Basso, K. *Wisdom Sits in Places: Landscape and Language Among Western Apache*. Albuquerque: University of New Mexico Press, 1996.

Behre, K. 'A New Holocene Sea-level Curve for the Southern North Sea', *Boreas* 36 (2007): 82–102.

Bell, M. *Prehistoric Coastal Communities: The Mesolithic in Western Britain*. York: Council for British Archaeology (CBA Research Report 149), 2007.

Bell, M. and M. J. C. Walker. *Late Quaternary Environmental Change. Physical and Human Perspectives*. Harlow: Pearson Education, 2005.

Bengtsson, L. 'Knowledge and Interaction in the Stone Age: Raw Materials for Adzes and Axes, Their Sources and Distributional Patterns', in L. Larsson (ed.), *Mesolithic on the Move: Papers Presented at the Sixth International Conference on the Mesolithic in Europe*, 388–94. Oxford: Oxbow Books, 2003.

Benjamin, J., C. Bonsall, C. Pickard and A. Fischer (eds). *Submerged Prehistory*. Oxford: Oxbow Books, 2011.

Bergsvik, K. A. 'Caught in the Middle: Functional and Ideological Aspects of Mesolithic Shores in Norway', in S. B. McCartan, R. Shulting, G. Warren and P. Woodman (eds), *Mesolithic Horizons*, 602–9. Oxford: Oxbow Books, 2009.

Bevan, L. and J. Moore (eds). *Peopling the Mesolithic in a Northern Environment*. Oxford: British Archaeological Report (BAR International Series 1157), 2003.

Binford, L. R. 'Post-Pleistocene Adaptations', in S. R. Binford and L. R. Binford (eds), *New Perspectives in Archaeology*, 313–41. Chicago: Aldine, 1968.

Bird, M. I., L. K. Fifield, T. S. Teh, C. H. Chang, N. Shirlaw and K. Lambeck. 'An Inflection in the Rate of Early Mid-Holocene Sea-level Rise: A New Sea-level Curve from Singapore', *Estuarine, Coastal and Shelf Science* 71 (2007): 523–36.

Blanchon, P. and J. Shaw. 'Reef Drowning During the Last Deglaciation: Evidence for Catastrophic Sea-level Rise and Ice-sheet Collapse', *Geology* 23 (1995): 4–8.

Bond, C. J. 'A Mesolithic Social Landscape in South-west Britain: The Somerset Levels and Mendip Hills', in S. B. McCartan, R. Shulting, G. Warren and P. Woodman (eds), *Mesolithic Horizons*, 706–16. Oxford: Oxbow Books, 2009.

Bondevik, S., F. Lovolt, C. Harbitz, J. Mangerud, A. Dawson and J. I. Svendsen. 'The Storegga Slide Tsunami – Comparing Field Observations with Numerical Observations', *Marine and Petroleum Geology* 22 (2005): 195–208.

Bonsall, C. 'The Mesolithic of the Iron Gates', in G. Bailey and P. Spikins (eds), *Mesolithic Europe*, 238–79. Cambridge: Cambridge University Press, 2008.

Bonsall, C., M. G. Macklin, R. W. Payton and A. Boroneanţ. 'Climate, Floods and River Gods: Environmental Change and the Meso-Neolithic Transition in South-east Europe', *Before Farming: The Archaeology of Old World Hunter-gatherers* 3–4 (2) (2002a): 1–15.

Bonsall, C., M. G. Macklin, D. E. Anderson and R. W. Payton. 'Climate Change and the Adoption of Agriculture in North-west Europe', *European Journal of Archaeology* 5 (2002b): 9–23.

Boomer, I., C. Waddington, T. Stevenson and D. Hamilton. 'Holocene Coastal Change and Geoarchaeology at Howick, Northumberland, UK', *The Holocene* 17 (1) (2007): 89–104.

Borić, D. and P. Miracle. 'Mesolithic and Neolithic (Dis)continuities in the Danube Gorges: New AMS Dates from Padina and Hajdučka Vodenica (Serbia)', *Oxford Journal of Archaeology* 23 (4) (2004): 341–71.

Bradley, R. 'Domestication as a State of Mind', *Analectia Praehistoria Leidensia* 29 (1997): 13–19.

Bradley, R. *An Archaeology of Natural Places*. London: Routledge, 2000.

Bradley, R. 'Domestication, Sedentism, Property and Time: Materiality
    and the Beginnings of Agriculture in Northern Europe', in E.
    DeMarrais, C. Gosden and C. Renfrew (eds), *Rethinking Materiality.*
    The Engagement of Mind with the Material World, 107–15. Cambridge:
    McDonald Institute for Archaeological Research (McDonald Institute
    Monographs), 2004.
Bradley, R. and B. Hooper. 'Recent Discoveries from Portsmouth and
    Langstone Harbours: Mesolithic to Iron Age', *Proceedings of the*
    Hampshire Field Club 30 (1975): 17–27.
Broadbent, N. D. and B. W. Edvinger. 'Sacred Sites, Settlements and Place-
    names: Ancient Saami Landscapes in Northern Coastal Sweden', in
    P. Jordan (ed.), *Landscape and Culture in Northern Eurasia*, 315–38.
    Walnut Creek, CA: Left Coast Press, 2011.
Brody, H. *The Other Side of Eden. Hunter-gatherers, Farmers, and the*
    Shaping of the World. London: Faber and Faber, 2001.
Brown, T. 'Divisions of Floodplain Space and Sites on Riverine "Islands":
    Functional, Ritual, Social, or Liminal Places?', *Journal of Wetland*
    Archaeology 3 (2003): 3–16.
Bruun, P. 'Sea-level Rise as a Cause of Shore Erosion', *Journal of the*
    Waterways and Harbors Division, American Society of Civil Engineers 88
    (1962): 117–30.
Bryant, E. A. and S. K. Haslett. 'Was the AD 1607 Coastal Flooding Event
    in the Severn Estuary and Bristol Channel (UK) Due to a Tsunami?',
    Archaeology in the Severn Estuary 13 (2002): 163–7.
Burkitt, M. C. 'A Maglemose Harpoon Dredged Up from the North Sea',
    Man 32 (1932): 99.
Callaghan, R. and C. Scarre. 'Simulating the Western Seaways', *Oxford*
    Journal of Archaeology 28 (2009): 357–72.
Cambrensis, G. *The Itinerary Through Wales: Descriptions of Wales*, 1908
    edn. London: Dent, Everyman, 1191.
Cameron, T. D. J., A. Crosby, P. S. Balson, D. H. Jeffery, G. K. Lott,
    J. Bulat and D. J. Harrison. *United Kingdom Offshore Regional Report:*
    The Geology of the Southern North Sea. London: HMSO (The British
    Geological Survey), 1992.
Case, H. 'Neolithic Explanations', *Antiquity* 43 (1969): 176–86.

Chatterton, R. 'Ritual', in C. Conneller and G. Warren (eds), *Mesolithic Britain and Ireland: New Approaches*, 101–20. Stroud: Tempus, 2006.

Childe, V. G. *What Happened in History*. Harmondsworth: Penguin Books, 1942.

Childe, V. G. *The Dawn of European Civilization*, 6th edn rev., first published 1925, this repr. 1973. St Albans: Paladin, 1957.

Childe, V. G. *The Prehistory of European Society*, 2009 repr. Nottingham: Spokesman, 1958.

Chu, H. 'Where Warming Hits Home', *Los Angeles Times*, 21 February 2007. Available from http://articles.latimes.com/2007/feb/21/world/fgwarming21 (accessed 16/10/2012).

Church, J. A., T. Aarup, P. L. Woodworth, W. S. Wilson, R. J. Nicholls, R. Ranor, K. Lambeck, G. T. Mitchum, K. Steffen, A. Cazenave, G. Blewitt, J. X. Mitrovica and J. A. Lowe. 'Sea-level Rise and Variability: Synthesis and Outlook for the Future', in J. A. Church, P. L. Woodworth, T. Aarup and W. S. Wilson (eds), *Understanding Sea-level Rise and Variability*, 402–19. Chichester: Wiley-Blackwell, 2010a.

Church, J. A., D. Roemmich, C. M. Domingues, J. K. Willis, N. J. White, J. E. Gilson, D. Stammer, A. Kohl, D. P. Chambers, F. W. Landerer, J. Marotzke, J. M. Gregory, T. Suzuki, A. Cazenave and P-Y. Le Traon. 'Ocean Temperature and Salinity Contributions to Global and Regional Sea-level Change', in J. A. Church, P. L. Woodworth, T. Aarup and W. S. Wilson (eds), *Understanding Sea-level Rise and Variability*, 143–76. Chichester: Wiley-Blackwell, 2010b.

Clark, C. D., A. L. C. Hughes, S. L. Greenwood, C. Jordan and H. P. Sejrup. 'Pattern and Timing of Retreat of the Last British-Irish Ice Sheet', *Quaternary Science Reviews* 44 (2012): 112–46.

Clark, J. G. D. *The Mesolithic Settlement of Northern Europe. A Case Study of the Food-gathering Peoples of Northern Europe During the Early Post-glacial Period*. Cambridge: Cambridge University Press, 1936.

Clark, J. G. D. 'Seal Hunting in the Stone Age of North-western Europe: A Study in Economic Prehistory', *Proceedings of the Prehistoric Society* 12 (1946): 12–48.

Clark, J. G. D. *Excavations at Star Carr*. Cambridge: Cambridge University Press, 1954.

Clark J. G. D. 'Excavations at the Neolithic Site at Hurst Fen, Mildenhall, Suffolk', *Proceedings of the Prehistoric Society* 26 (1960): 202–24.

Clark, J. G. D. *The Earlier Stone Age Settlement of Scandinavia*. Cambridge: Cambridge University Press, 1975.

Clark J. G. D. and H. Godwin. 'The Neolithic in the Cambridgeshire Fens', *Antiquity* 36 (1962): 10–23.

Clark, J. G. D. and W. F. Rankine. 'Excavations at Farnham, Surrey (1937–38): The Horsham Culture and the Question of Mesolithic Dwellings', *Proceedings of the Prehistoric Society* 5 (1) (1939): 61–118.

Clarke, G. K. C., D. W. Leverington, J. T. Teller and A. S. Dyke. 'Paleohydraulics of the Last Outburst Flood from Glacial Lake Agassiz and the 8200 BP Cold Event', *Quaternary Science Reviews* 23 (2004): 389–407.

Coles, B. J. 'Doggerland: A Speculative Survey', *Proceedings of the Prehistoric Society* 64 (1998): 45–81.

Coles, B. J. 'Doggerland's Loss and the Neolithic', in B. Coles, J. Coles and M. Schon Jørgensen (eds), *Bog Bodies, Sacred Sites and Wetland Archaeology*, 51–7. Exeter: WARP (Occasional Paper 12), 1999.

Coles, B. J. 'Doggerland: The Cultural Dynamics of a Shifting Coastline', in K. Pye and J. R. Allen (eds), *Coastal and Estuarine Environments: Sedimentology, Geomorphology and Geoarchaeology*, 393–401. London: Geological Society (Geological Society Special Publications 175), 2000.

Coles, B. J. 'Reminiscences of a Wetland Archaeologist', in F. Menotti and A. O'Sullivan (eds), *The Oxford Handbook of Wetland Archaeology*, 903–19. Oxford: Oxford University Press, 2013.

Conneller, C. (ed.). *New Approaches to the Palaeolithic and Mesolithic*. Cambridge: Archaeological Review from Cambridge 17 (1) (2000).

Conneller, C. 'Becoming Deer. Corporeal Transformations at Star Carr', *Archaeological Dialogues* 11 (1) (2004): 37–56.

Conneller, C. 'Death', in C. Conneller and G. Warren (eds), *Mesolithic Britain and Ireland: New Approaches*, 139–64. Stroud: Tempus, 2006.

Conneller, C. and T. Schadla-Hall. 'Beyond Star Carr: The Vale of Pickering in the 10th Millennium BP', *Proceedings of the Prehistoric Society* 69 (2003): 85–106.

Conneller, C. and G. Warren (eds). *Mesolithic Britain and Ireland: New Approaches*. Stroud: Tempus, 2006.

Conneller, C., N. Milner, B. Taylor and M. Taylor. 'Substantial Settlement in the European Early Mesolithic: New Research at Star Carr', *Antiquity* 86 (2012): 1004–20.

Conneller, C., M. Bates, T. Schadla-Hall, J. Coles, M. Pope, B. Scott and A. Shaw. 'The Mesolithic of the Channel Islands', *Proceedings of the Prehistoric Society* 81, planned for 2015.

Cooper, J. 'Fail to Prepare, then Prepare to Fail: Rethinking Threat, Vulnerability, and Mitigation in the Precolumbian Caribbean', in J. Cooper and P. Sheets (eds), *Surviving Sudden Environmental Change. Answers from Archaeology*, 91–115. Boulder, CO: Colorado University Press, 2012.

Costello, A., M. Abbas, A. Allen, S. Ball, S. Bell, R. Bellamy, S. Friel, N. Groce, A. Johnson, M. Kett, M. Lee, C. Levy, M. Maslin, D. McCoy, B. McGuire, H. Montgomery, D. Napier, C. Pagel, J. Patel, J. Antonio, P. de Oliveira, H. Rees, D. Rogger, J. Scott, J. Stephenson, J. Twigg, J. Wolff and C. Patterson. 'Managing the Health Effects of Climate Change', *Lancet* 373 (2009): 1693–733.

Crombé, P. 'The Wetlands of Sandy Flanders (Northwest Belgium): Potentials and Prospects for Prehistoric Research and Management', in E. Rensink and H. Peeters (eds), *Preserving the Early Past: Investigation, Selection and Preservation of Palaeolithic and Mesolithic Sites and Landscapes*, 41–54. Amersfoort: Rijksdienst voor het Oudheidkundig Bodermonderzoek, 2006.

Crombé, P., J. Sergant, E. Robinson and J. de Reu. 'Hunter-gatherer Responses to Environmental Change During the Pleistocene–Holocene Transition in the Southern North Sea Basin: Final Palaeolithic–Final Mesolithic Land Use in Northwest Belgium', *Journal of Anthropological Archaeology* 30 (2011): 454–71.

Damasio, A. *The Feeling of What Happens: Body and Emotion in the Making of Consciousness*. London: Vintage Books, 1999.

Damasio, A. *Looking for Spinoza: Joy, Sorrow, and the Feeling of the Brain*. London: Vintage Books, 2003.

Damasio, A. *Self Comes to Mind. Constructing the Conscious Brain*. London: Vintage Books, 2012.

Dark, P., T. F. G. Higham, R. Jacobi and T. C. Lord. 'New Radiocarbon Accelerator Dates on Artefacts from the Early Mesolithic Site of Star Carr, North Yorkshire', *Archaeometry* 48 (1) (2006): 185–200.

Davis, I. and N. Hall, 'Ways to Measure Community Vulnerability', in J. Ingleton (ed.), *Natural Disaster Management*, 87–9. Leicester: Tudor Rose, 1999.

Dawson, A., D. Smith and D. Long. 'Evidence for a Tsunami from a Mesolithic Site in Inverness, Scotland', *Journal of Archaeological Science* 17 (1990): 509–12.

Digerfeldt, G. 'Reconstruction and Regional Correlation of Holocene Lake-level Fluctuations in Lake Bysjön, South Sweden', *Boreas* 17 (1988): 165–82.

Dix, J. K. and F. Sturt. *The Relic Palaeo-landscapes of the Thames Estuary.* Southampton: Southampton University (MALSF Open Report 09/ P126), 2011.

Douglas, B. C. 'An Introduction to Sea-level', in B. C. Douglas, M. S. Kearney and S. P. Leatherman (eds), *Sea-level Rise. History and Consequences*, 1–11. London: Academic Press (International Geophysics Series 75), 2001.

Douglas, M. *Purity and Danger.* London: Routledge, 1966.

Draper, J. C. 'Mesolithic Distribution in South-east Hampshire', *Proceedings of the Hampshire Field Club* 23 (1968): 110–19.

Ducrocq, T. *Le Mésolithique du Bassin de la Somme. Insertion dans un Cadre Morphostratigraphique, Environnemental et Chrono-culturel.* Lille: Publications du CERP (No. 7, Université des sciences et technologies de Lille, 255), 2001.

Ducrocq, T., A. Bridault and S. Coutard. 'Le Gisement Mesolithique de Warluis (Oise). Approche Préliminaire', in J-P. Fagnart, A. Thevenin, T. Ducrocq, B. Souffi and P. Coudret (eds), *Le Début du Mésolithique en Europe du Nord-Ouest*, 85–106. Paris: Mémoires de la Société Préhistorique Française 45, 2008.

Duggan, P. D. *Villager Participation in the Relocation of El Gourna, Egypt.* London: Royal Institution of Chartered Surveyors (RICS) research report, 2012.

Echo-Hawk, R. C. 'Ancient History in the New World: Integrating Oral

Traditions and the Archaeological Record in Deep Time', *American Antiquity* 65 (2) (2000): 267–90.

Edenmo, R. 'From Sharing to Giving: Handling the Inequality of Things at the End of the Mesolithic', in S. B. McCartan, R. Shulting, G. Warren and P. Woodman (eds), *Mesolithic Horizons*, 737–40. Oxford: Oxbow Books, 2009.

Eren, M. I. *Hunter-gatherer Behavior. Human Response During the Younger Dryas*. California: Left Coast Press, 2012.

Evans, J. G. *Environmental Archaeology and Social Order*. London: Routledge, 2003.

Fairbanks, R. G. 'A 17,000-year Old Glacio-eustatic Sea-level Record: Influence of Glacial Melting Rates on the Younger Dryas Event and Deep-ocean Circulation', *Nature* 342 (1989): 637–42.

Fairbridge, R. W. 'Isostasy and Eustasy', in D. E. Smith and A. G. Dawson (eds), *Shorelines and Isostasy*, 3–25. London: Academic Press, 1983.

Few, R., M. Ahern, F. Matthies and S. Kovats. *Floods, Health and Climate Change: A Strategic Review*. Norwich: University of East Anglia (Tyndall Centre for Climate Change Research, Working Paper 63), 2004a.

Few, R., G. T. Pham and T. T. H. Bui. *Living with Floods: Health Risks and Coping Strategies of the Urban Poor in Vietnam*. Norwich: University of East Anglia (Research Report), 2004b.

Field, D. *Use of Land in Central Southern England During the Neolithic and Early Bronze Age*. Oxford: British Archaeology Report (BAR British Series 458), 2008.

Fischer, A. 'Submerged Stone Age – Danish Examples and North Sea Potential', in N. C. Flemming (ed.), *Submarine Prehistoric Archaeology of the North Sea. Research Priorities and Collaboration with Industry*, 23–36. York: Council for British Archaeology/English Heritage (CBA Research Report 141), 2004.

Fitch, S. 'The Mesolithic Landscape of the Southern North Sea'. PhD thesis, University of Birmingham, 2011.

Fitch, S., K. Thomson and V. Gaffney. 'Late Pleistocene and Holocene Depositional Systems and the Palaeogeography of the Dogger Bank, North Sea', *Quaternary Research* 64 (2005): 185–96.

Fitch, S., V. Gaffney and K. Thomson. 'The Archaeology of the North

Sea Palaeolandscapes', in V. Gaffney, K. Thomson and S. Fitch (eds), *Mapping Doggerland. The Mesolithic Landscapes of the Southern North Sea*, 105–18. Oxford: Archaeopress (BAR 31), 2007.

Fitzhugh, B. 'Hazards, Impacts, and Resilience Among Hunter-gatherers of the Kuril Islands', in J. Cooper and P. Sheets (eds), *Surviving Sudden Environmental Change. Answers from Archaeology*, 19–42. Boulder, CO: Colorado University Press, 2012.

Flemming, N. C. *The Scope of Strategic Environmental Assessment of North Sea Areas SEA3 and SEA2 in Regard to Prehistoric Archaeological Remains*. Department of Trade and Industry, Report TR_014, 2002.

Flemming, N. C. (ed). *Submarine Prehistoric Archaeology of the North Sea. Research Priorities and Collaboration with Industry*. York: Council for British Archaeology/English Heritage (CBA Research Report 141), 2004.

Fletcher, C. R. L. and R. Kipling. *A History of England*. Oxford: Henry Frowde and Hodder & Stoughton, 1911.

Flood, J. *Archaeology of the Dreamtime: The Story of Prehistoric Australia and its People*. Sydney: Collins, 1983.

Fox, S. 'These are Things that are Really Happening: Inuit Perspectives on the Evidence and Impacts of Climate Change in Nunavut', in I. Krupnik and D. Jolly (eds), *The Earth is Faster Now: Indigenous Observations of Arctic Environmental Change*, 13–53. Fairbanks, AK: Arctic Research Consortium of the United States, 2002.

Furgal, C., D. Martin and P. Gosselin. 'Climate Change and Health in Nunavik and Labrador: Lessons from Inuit Knowledge', in I. Krupnik and D. Jolly (eds), *The Earth is Faster Now: Indigenous Observations of Arctic Environmental Change*, 266–99. Fairbanks, AK: Arctic Research Consortium of the United States, 2002.

Gaffney, V., K. Thomson and S. Fitch (eds). *Mapping Doggerland. The Mesolithic Landscapes of the Southern North Sea*. Oxford: Archaeopress (British Archaeological Reports 31), 2007.

Gaffney, V., S. Fitch and D. Smith. *Europe's Lost World. The Rediscovery of Doggerland*. York: Council for British Archaeology (CBA Research Report 160), 2009.

Garnett, E. R., J. E. Andrews, R. C. Preece and P. F. Dennis. 'Climatic Change Recorded by Stable Isotopes and Trace Elements in a

British Holocene Tufa', *Journal of Quaternary Science* 19 (3) (2004): 251–62.

Garrow, D. and Sturt, F. 'Grey Waters Bright with Neolithic Argonauts? Maritime Connections and the Mesolithic-Neolithic Transition Within the 'Western Seaways' of Britain, c. 5000–3500 BC', *Antiquity* 85 (2011): 59–72.

Gbetibouo, G. A. *Understanding Farmers' Perceptions and Adaptations to Climate Change and Variability. The Case of the Limpopo Basin, South Africa*. International Food Policy Research Institute, IFPRI discussion paper 00849, Environment and Production Technology Division (E-book), 2009.

Gearey, B. R., S. Griffiths, E. J. Hopla and D. R. Tappin. 'Methodological and Interpretative Issues for Integrated Palaeoenvironmental and Archaeological Investigations of Submerged Landscapes: A Case Study from the Southern North Sea', in V. Gaffney (ed.), *Between the Salt Water and the Sea Strand: Comparative Methodologies in Submerged Landscape Research*. Oxford: Oxbow Books, planned for 2015.

Gendel, P. A. *Mesolithic Social Territories in Northwestern Europe*. Oxford: British Archaeological Report (BAR International Series 218), 1984.

Ghesquière, E. and G. Marchand. *Le Mésolithique en France*. Paris: La Decouverte, 2010.

Ghesquière, E., P. Lefèvre, C. Marcigny and B. Souffi. *Le Mésolithique Moyen du Nord-Cotentin Basse-Normandie, France*. Oxford: British Archaeology Report (BAR International Series 856), 2000.

Gibson, E. and A. Pick. *An Ecological Approach to Perceptual Learning and Development*. Oxford: Oxford University Press, 2000.

Glimerveen, J., D. Mol, K. Post, J. W. F. Reumer, H. van der Plicht, B. van Geel, G. van Reenan and J. P. Pals. 'The North Sea Project. The First Palaeontological, Palynological and Archaeological Results', in N. C. Flemming (ed.), *Submarine Prehistoric Archaeology of the North Sea. Research Priorities and Collaboration with Industry*, 21–36. York: Council for British Archaeology/English Heritage (CBA Research Report 141), 2004.

Godwin, H. 'Coastal Peat Beds of the British Isles and North Sea', *Journal of Ecology* 31 (1943): 199.

Gosden, C. 'Aesthetics, Intelligence and Emotions: Implications for Archaeology', in E. DeMarrais, C. Gosden and C. Renfrew (eds), *Rethinking Materiality. The Engagement of Mind with the Material World*, 33–40. Cambridge: McDonald Institute for Archaeological Research (McDonald Institute Monographs), 2004.

Gratton, J. 'Aspect of Armageddon: An Exploration of the Role of Volcanic Eruptions in Human History and Civilization', *Quaternary International* 151 (2006): 10–18.

Green, M. *A Landscape Revealed: 10,000 Years on a Chalkland Farm.* Stroud: Tempus, 2000.

Grimaldi, S. and E. Flor. 'From the Mountain to the Sea: An Ethnographic Perspective for the Early Mesolithic Settlement Dynamics in Northeastern Italy', in S. B. McCartan, R. Shulting, G. Warren and P. Woodman (eds), *Mesolithic Horizons*, 754–9. Oxford: Oxbow Books, 2009.

Grøn, O. and J. Skaarup. 'Mollegabet II – a Submerged Mesolithic Site and "Boat Burial"', *Journal of Danish Archaeology* 10 (1991): 38–50.

Grøn, O. and J. Skaarup. 'Submerged Stone Age Coastal Zones in Denmark: Investigation Strategies and Results', in N. C. Flemming (ed.), *Submarine Prehistoric Archaeology of the North Sea. Research Priorities and Collaboration with Industry*, 53–6. York: English Heritage/Council for British Archaeology (CBA Research Report 141), 2004a.

Grøn, O. and J. Skaarup. *Mollegabet II: A Submerged Mesolithic Settlement in Southern Denmark.* Oxford: Archaeopress (BAR International Series 1328), 2004b.

Grothman, T. and A. Patt. 'Adaptive Capacity and Human Cognition: The Process of Individual Adaptation to Climate Change', *Global Environment Change* 15 (3) (2005): 199–213.

Gupta, S., P. Collier, A. Palmer-Felgate, J. Dickinson, K. Bushe and S. Humber. *Submerged Palaeo-Arun River: Reconstruction of Prehistoric Landscapes and Evaluation of Archaeological Resource Potential. Integrated Projects 1&2. Unpublished Final Report for English Heritage.* Salisbury: Wessex Archaeology, 2004.

Gupta, S., J. Collier, A. Palmer-Felgate and G. Potter. 'Catastrophic Flooding Origin of Shelf Valley Systems in the English Channel', *Nature* 448 (2007): 342–6.

Haines, A., R. S. Kovats, D. Campbell-Lendrum and C. Corvalan. 'Climate Change and Human Health: Impacts, Vulnerability, and Mitigation', *Lancet* 367 (2006): 2101–9.

Hansen, J. E. 'A Slippery Slope: How Much Global Warming Constitutes "Dangerous Anthropogenic Interface". An Editorial Essay', *Climate Change* 68 (2005): 269–79.

Hardy, K. and C. R. Wickham-Jones. 'Mesolithic and Later Sites Around the Inner Sound, Scotland: The Work of the Scotland's First Settlers Project 1998–2004', *Scottish Archaeological Internet Reports* 31, 2009. Available from http://www.sair.org.uk/sair31/ (accessed 11/02/2013).

Harris, M. *Life on the Amazon: The Anthropology of a Brazilian Peasant Village*. Oxford: Oxford University Press, 2000.

Harris, M. 'Rhythm of Wetland Life. Seasonality and Sociality', in F. Menotti and A. O'Sullivan (eds), *The Oxford Handbook of Wetland Archaeology*, 749–60. Oxford: Oxford University Press, 2013.

Haslett, S. K. and E. A. Bryant. 'The AD 1607 Coastal Flood in the Bristol Channel and Severn Estuary: Historical Records from Devon and Cornwall (UK)', *Archaeology in the Severn Estuary* 15 (2004): 81–9.

Hickling, R. *The Effect of Climate Change on the Distribution, Phenology and Abundance of British Plants and Animals*. PhD thesis, University of York, 2006.

Hijma, M. P. and K. M. Cohen. 'Timing and Magnitude of the Sea-level Jump Preluding the 8200 yr Event', *Geology* 38 (3) (2010): 275–8.

Hijma, M. P. and K. M. Cohen. 'Holocene Transgression of the Rhine River Mouth Area, The Netherlands/Southern North Sea: Palaeogeography and Sequence Stratigraphy', *Sedimentology* 58 (2011): 1453–85.

Hind, D. 'Picking up the Trail: People, Landscapes and Technology in the Peak District of Derbyshire During the Fifth and Fourth Millennia BC', in A. M. Chadwick (ed.), *Stories from the Landscape: Archaeologies of Inhabitation*, 130–76. Oxford: British Archaeological Reports (BAR International Series 1238), 2004.

Hoffman, S. 'The Monster and the Mother: The Symbolism of Disaster', in S. Hoffman and A. Oliver-Smith (eds), *Catastrophe and Culture: The Anthropology of Disaster*, 113–41. Santa Fe: School of American Research Press, 2002.

Holford, S., K. Thomson and V. Gaffney. 'Salt Tectonics in the Southern North Sea: Controls on Late Pleistocene-Holocene Geomorphology', in V. Gaffney, K. Thomson and S. Fitch (eds), *Mapping Doggerland. The Mesolithic Landscapes of the Southern North Sea*, 61–5. Oxford: Archaeopress (BAR 31), 2007.

Horton, R., C. Herweijer, C., Rosenzweig, J. Liu, V. Gornitz and A. C. Ruane. 'Sea-level Rise Projections for Current Generation CGMs Based on the Semi-empirical Method', *Geophysical Research Letters* 35, L02715 (2008).

Hsu, C-Y. 'Chinese Attitudes Towards Climate', in R. J. McIntosh, J. A. Tainter and S. K. McIntosh (eds), *The Way the Wind Blows. Climate, History, and Human Action*, 209–19. New York: Columbia University Press, 2000.

Huang, E. and J. Tian. 'Melt-Water-Pulse (MWP) Events and Abrupt Climate Change of the Last Deglaciation', *Chinese Science Bulletin* 53 (18) (2008): 2867–78.

Huntley, B. and H. J. B. Birks. *An Atlas of Past and Present Pollen Maps of Europe 0–13,000 Years Ago*. Cambridge: Cambridge University Press, 1983.

Ingold, T. *The Perception of the Environment. Essays in Livelihood, Dwelling and Skill*. Abingdon: Routledge, 2000.

Ingold, T. and T. Kurtilla. 'Perceiving the Environment in Finnish Lapland', *Body & Society* 6 (3–4) (2000): 183–96.

Jacobi, R. 'The Mesolithic of Sussex', in P. L. Drewett (ed.), *Archaeology in Sussex to AD 1500*, 15–22. London: The Council for British Archaeology (Research Report No. 29), 1978.

Jacobi, R. M. 'Early Flandrian Hunters in the South-west', *Proceedings of the Devon Archaeological Society* 37 (1979): 48–93.

James, J. W. C., B. Pearce, R. A. Coggan, S. H. L. Arnott, R. W. E. Clark, J. F. Plim, J. Pinnion, C. Barrio Frójan, J. P. Gardiner, A. Morando, P. A. Baggaley, G. Scott and N. Bigourdan. *The South Coast Regional Environmental Characterisation*. British Geological Survey Open Report OR/09/51, 2010.

James, J. W. C., B. Pearce, R. A. Coggan, M. Leivers, R. W. E. Clark, J. F. Plim, J. M. Hill, S. H. L. Arnott, L. Bateson, A. De-Burgh Thomas and P. A. Baggaley. *The MALSF Synthesis Study in the Central and Eastern English Channel.* British Geological Survey Open Report OR/11/01, 2011.

Jelgersma, S. 'Holocene Sea-level Changes in the Netherlands', *Mededelingen van de Geologishe Stichting* (Serie C, no. 6–7) (1961): 1–100.

Jelgersma, S. 'Sea-level Changes in the North Sea Basin', in E. Oerle, R. T. E. Shuttenhelm and A. J. Wiggers (eds), *The Quaternary History of the North Sea*, 233–48. Symposia Universitatis Upsaliensis Annum Quingentesimum Celebrantis 2, 1979.

Johansson, A. D. *Stoksbjerg Vest. Et Senpalaeolitisk Fundkompleks ved Porsmose, Sydsjaelland. Fra Bromme – til Ahrensburgkultur i Norden.* Sweden: Nordiske Fortidsminder (Serie C, Bind 3), 2003.

Johnson, H., P. C. Richards, D. Long and C. C. Graham. *The Geology of the Northern North Sea.* London: Her Majesty's Stationery Office, 1993.

Johnson, J. R. 'Social Responses to Climate Change Among the Chumash Indians of South-central California', in R. J. McIntosh, J. A. Tainter and S. K. McIntosh (eds), *The Way the Wind Blows. Climate, History, and Human Action*, 301–27. New York: Columbia University Press, 2000.

Johnson, M. *The Meaning of the Body. Aesthetics of Human Understanding.* Chicago: University of Chicago Press, 2007.

Johnston, P. 'The Role of Hydro-isostasy for Holocene Sea-level Changes in the British Isles', *Marine Geology* 124 (1995): 61–70.

Jolly, D., F. Berkes, J. Castleden, T. Nichols and the community of Sachs Harbour. 'We Can't Predict the Weather Like we Used to: Inuvialuit Observations of Climate Change, Sachs Harbour, Western Canadian Arctic', in I. Krupnik and D. Jolly (eds), *The Earth is Faster Now: Indigenous Observations of Arctic Environmental Change*, 93–125. Fairbanks, AK: Arctic Research Consortium of the United States, 2002.

Jones, O. '"The Breath of the Moon": The Rhythmic and Affective Time-spaces of UK Tides', in T. Edensor (ed.), *Geographies of Rhythm. Nature, Place, Mobilities and Bodies*, 189–203. Farnham: Ashgate Publishing, 2010.

Jordan, P. (ed.). *Landscape and Culture in Northern Eurasia*. Walnut Creek, CA: Left Coast Press, 2011.

Joughin, I., W. Abdalati and M. Fahnestock. 'Large Fluctuations in Speed on Greenland's Jakobshavn Isbrae Glacier', *Nature* 432 (2004): 608–10.

Kearney, M. S. 'Late Holocene Sea-level Variation', in B. Douglas, M. Kearney and S. Leatherman (eds), *Sea-level Rise. History and Consequences*, 13–36. London: Academic Press (International Geophysics Series 75), 2001.

Kearney, M. S. and J. C. Stevenson. 'Island Land Loss and Marsh Vertical Accretion Rate: Evidence for Historical Sea-level Changes in Chesapeake Bay', *Journal of Coastal Research* 7 (1991): 403–15.

Keith, S. A. *Impacts of Environmental Change on Ecological Communities*. PhD thesis, Bournemouth University, 2010.

Kelly, R. L. 'Colonization of New Land by Hunter-gatherers. Expectations and Implications Based on Ethnographic Data', in M. Rockman and J. Steele (eds), *Colonization of Unfamiliar Landscapes: The Archaeology of Adaptation*, 44–58. London: Routledge, 2003.

Kiden, P., L. Denys and P. Johnston. 'Late Quaternary Sea-level Change and Isostatic and Tectonic Land Movement Along the Belgian-Dutch North Sea Coast: Geological Data and Model Results', *Journal of Quaternary Science* 17 (2002): 535–46.

Kind, C-J. 'Transport of Lithic Raw Material in the Mesolithic of Southwest Germany', *Journal of Anthropological Archaeology* 25 (2006): 213–25.

Kolfschoten, T. van and H. van Essen. 'Palaeozoological Heritage from the Bottom of the North Sea', in N. C. Flemming (ed.), *Submarine Prehistoric Archaeology of the North Sea. Research Priorities and Collaboration with Industry*, 70–80. York: English Heritage/Council for British Archaeology (CBA Research Report 141), 2004.

Krajick, K. 'Tracking Myth to Geological Reality', *Science* 310 (5749) (2005): 762–4.

Krupnik, I. 'Watching Ice and Weather Our Way: Some Lessons From Yupik Observations of Sea Ice and Weather on St. Lawrence Island, Alaska', in I. Krupnik and D. Jolly (eds), *The Earth is Faster Now: Indigenous Observations of Arctic Environmental Change*, 156–99. Fairbanks, AK: Arctic Research Consortium of the United States, 2002.

Krupnik, I. and D. Jolly (eds). *The Earth is Faster Now: Indigenous Observations of Arctic Environmental Change.* Fairbanks, AK: Arctic Research Consortium of the United States, 2002.

Kvamme, K. and M. A. Jochim. 'The Environmental Basis of Mesolithic Settlement', in C. Bonsall (ed.), *The Mesolithic in Europe: Proceedings of the Third International Symposium, Edinburgh 1985,* 1–12. Edinburgh: John Donald, 1989.

Lambeck, K. 'Late Devensian and Holocene Shorelines of the British Isles and North Sea from Models of Glacio-hydro-isostatic Rebound', *Journal of the Geological Society, London* 152 (1995): 437–48.

Lambeck, K., C. D. Woodroffe, F. Antonioli, M. Anzidei, W. R. Gehrels, J. Laborel and A. Wright. 'Palaeoenvironmental Records, Geophysical Modelling, and Reconstruction of Sea-level Trends and Variability on Centennial and Longer Timescales', in J. A. Church, P. L. Woodworth, T. Aarup and W. S. Wilson (eds), *Understanding Sea-level Rise and Variability,* 61–121. Chichester: Wiley-Blackwell, 2010.

Larsson, L. *The Skateholm Project I: Man and Environment.* Stockholm: Almqvist and Wiksell International, 1988a.

Larsson, L. 'Aspects of Exchange in Mesolithic Societies', in B. Hårdh, L. Larsson, D. Olausson and R. Petré (eds), *Trade and Exchange in Prehistory. Studies in Honour of Berta Stjernquist,* 25–32. Lund: Almqvist and Wiksell International (Acta Archaeologica Lundensia 8 (16)), 1988b.

Larsson, L. 'The Mesolithic of Southern Scandinavia', *Journal of World Prehistory* 4 (3) (1990a): 257–309.

Larsson, L. 'Dogs in Fraction – Symbols in Action', in P. Vermeersch and P. van Peer (eds), *Contributions to the Mesolithic in Europe,* 161–7. Leuven: Leuven University Press, 1990b.

Larsson, L. 'Introduction (Ritual and Symbolic Session)', in L. Larsson, H. Kindgren, K. Knutsson, D. Loeffler and A. Åkerlund (eds), *Mesolithic on the Move,* 463–6. Oxford: Oxbow Books, 2003.

Leatherman, S. P. 'Social and Economic Cost of Sea-level Rise', in B. Douglas, M. Kearney and S. Leatherman (eds), *Sea-level Rise. History and Consequences,* 181–223. London: Academic Press (International Geophysics Series 75), 2001.

Limpenny, S. E., C. Barrio Froján, C. Cotterill, R. L. Foster-Smith,
B. Pearce, L. Tizzard, D. L. Limpenny, D. Long, S. Walmsley, S. Kirby,
K. Baker, W. J. Meadows, J. Rees, J. Hill, C. Wilson, M. Leivers,
S. Churchley, J. Russell, A. C. Birchenough, S. L. Green and R. J. Law.
The East Coast Regional Environmental Characterisation. CEFAS Open
Report 08/04, 2011.

Long, A. J. 'Coastal Responses to Changes in Sea-level in the East Kent
Fens and Southeast England, UK Over the last 7500 Years', *Proceedings
of the Geologists' Association* 103 (1992): 187–99.

Long, A. J., A. J. Plater, M. Waller and J. B. Innes. 'Holocene Coastal
Sedimentation in the Eastern English Channel: New Data From the
Romney Marsh Region, United Kingdom', *Marine Geology* 136 (1996):
97–120.

Long, D., D. E. Smith and A. G. Dawson. 'A Holocene Tsunami Deposit in
Eastern Scotland', *Journal of Quaternary Science* 4 (1989): 61–6.

Louwe Kooijmans, L. P. 'The Hardinxveld Sites in the Rhine/Meuse Delta,
The Netherlands, 5500–4500 cal BC', in L. Larsson, H. Kindgren,
K. Knutsson, D. Loeffler and A. Åkerlund (eds), *Mesolithic on the Move*,
608–24. Oxford: Oxbow Books, 2003.

Lowe, J. A., P. L. Woodworth, T. Knutson, R. E. McDonald, K. L. McInnes,
K. Woth, H. von Storch, J. Wolf, V. Swail, B. Bernier, S. Gulev, K. J.
Horsburgh, A. S. Unnikrishnan, J. R. Hunter and R. Weisse. 'Past and
Future Changes in Extreme Sea-levels and Waves', in J. A. Church, P. L.
Woodworth, T. Aarup and W. S. Wilson (eds), *Understanding Sea-level
Rise and Variability*, 326–75. Chichester: Wiley-Blackwell, 2010.

Lubbock, J. (Lord Avebury). *Pre-historic Times, as Illustrated by Ancient
Remains, and the Manners and Customs of Modern Savages*, 7th edn.
London: Williams and Norgate, 1913.

Lübke, H. 'New Investigations on Submarine Stone Age Settlements in the
Wismar Bay Area', in L. Larsson, H. Kindgren, K. Knutsson, D. Loeffler
and A. Åkerlund (eds), *Mesolithic on the Move*, 633–42. Oxford: Oxbow
Books, 2003.

Lübke, H. 'Hunters and Fishers in a Changing World. Investigations
on Submerged Stone Age Sites off the Baltic Coast of Mecklenburg-
Vorpommern, Germany', in S. B. McCartan, R. Shulting, G. Warren and

P. Woodman (eds), *Mesolithic Horizons*, 556–60. Oxford: Oxbow Books, 2009.

Lübke, H., U. Schmölcke and F. Tauber. 'Mesolithic Hunter-fishers in a Changing World: A Case Study of Submerged Sites on the Jäckelberg, Wismar Bay, Northeastern Germany', in J. Benjamin, C. Bonsall, C. Pickard and A. Fischer (eds), *Submerged Prehistory*, 21–37. Oxford: Oxbow Books, 2011.

Maarleveld, T. J. and H. Peeters. 'Can we Manage?', in N. C. Flemming (ed.), *Submarine Prehistoric Archaeology of the North Sea. Research Priorities and Collaboration with Industry*, 102–12. York: English Heritage/Council for British Archaeology (CBA Research Report 141), 2004.

Macklin, M. and J. Lewin. 'River Sediments, Great Floods and Centennial-scale Holocene Climate Change', *Journal of Quaternary Science* 18 (2003): 101–5.

Macklin, M., C. Bonsall, F. M. Davies and M. Robinson. 'Human–Environment Interactions During the Holocene: New Data and Interpretations From the Oban Area, Argyll, Scotland', *The Holocene* 10 (2000): 109–21.

Magny, M. 'Holocene Climate Variability as Reflected by Mid-European Lake-level Fluctuations and its Probable Impact on Prehistoric Settlements', *Quaternary International* 113 (2004): 65–79.

Mannino, M. A. and K. D. Thomas. 'The Tragedy of the Shoreline? Social Ecology of Mesolithic Coastal Subsistence, with Reference to the Site of Culverwell, Isle of Portland (Southern England)', in S. B. McCartan, R. Shulting, G. Warren and P. Woodman (eds), *Mesolithic Horizons*, 146–51. Oxford: Oxbow Books, 2009.

Marchand, G. 'Les Occupations Mésolithiques a l'Intérieur du Finistère. Bilan Archéographie et Méthodologique (2001–2003)', *Revue Archéologique de l'Ouest* 22 (2005): 25–84.

Marchand, G. 'Et Maintenant, Qu'est-ce Qu'on Fait? Le Mésolithique de l'Ouest, 80 Ans Après M. et St.-J. Péquart', in *Marthe et Saint-Just Péquart, Archéologues des îles. De Houat à Hoëdic, 1923-1934*, 213–28. Melvan: La Revue des deux îles, 4, 2007.

Matthiessen, T. *George Catlin's North American Indians*. London: Penguin Books, 1989.

Mayewski, P. A., E. E. Rohling, J. C. Stager, W. Karlén, K. A. Maasch,
L. D. Meeker, E. A. Meyerson, F. Gasse, S. van Kreveld, K. Holmgren,
J. Lee-Thorp, G. Rosqvist, F. Rack, M. Staubwasser, R. R. Schneider
and E. J. Steig. 'Holocene Climate Variability', *Quaternary Research* 62
(2004): 243–55.

McIntosh, R. J., J. A. Tainter and S. K. McIntosh. 'Climate, History, and
Human Action', in R. J. McIntosh, J. A. Tainter and S. K. McIntosh (eds),
The Way the Wind Blows. Climate, History, and Human Action, 121–40.
New York: Columbia University Press, 2000.

McMichael, A. J., R. E. Woodruff and S. Hales. 'Climate Change and
Human Health: Present and Future Risks', *Lancet* 367 (2006): 859–69.

McQuade, M. and L. O'Donnell. 'Late Mesolithic Fish Traps From the
Liffey Estuary, Dublin, Ireland', *Antiquity* 81 (313) (2007): 569–84.

McQuade, M. and L. O'Donnell. 'The Excavation of Late Mesolithic
Fish Trap Remains From the Liffey Estuary, Dublin, Ireland', in S. B.
McCartan, R. Shulting, G. Warren and P. Woodman (eds), *Mesolithic
Horizons*, 889–94. Oxford: Oxbow Books, 2009.

McRobie, A., T. Spencer and H. Gerritsen. 'The Big Flood: North Sea Storm
Surge', *Philosophical Transactions of the Royal Society* A 363 (2005):
1263–70.

Mellars, P. A. *Excavations on Oronsay: Prehistoric Human Ecology on a
Small Island*. Edinburgh: Edinburgh University Press, 1987.

Menotti, F. *Wetland Archaeology and Beyond. Theory and Practice*. Oxford:
Oxford University Press, 2012.

Milner, N. 'Subsistence', in C. Conneller and G. Warren (eds),
Mesolithic Britain and Ireland: New Approaches, 61–82. Stroud: Tempus,
2006.

Milner, N. and E. Laurie. 'Coastal Perspectives on the Mesolithic–
Neolithic Transition', in S. B. McCartan, R. Shulting, G. Warren and
P. Woodman (eds), *Mesolithic Horizons*, 134–9. Oxford: Oxbow Books,
2009.

Milner, N. and P. Woodman (eds). *Mesolithic Studies at the Beginning of the
21st Century*. Oxford: Oxbow Books, 2005.

Minc, L. D. and K. P. Smith. 'The Spirit of Survival: Cultural Responses to
Resource Variability in North Alaska', in P. Halstead and J. O'Shea (eds),

Bad Year Economics. Cultural Responses to Risk and Uncertainty, 8–39. Cambridge: Cambridge University Press, 1989.

Mithen, S. *Thoughtful Foragers. A Study of Prehistoric Decision Making.* Cambridge: Cambridge University Press, 1990.

Mithen, S. 'A Cybernetic Wasteland'? Rationality, Emotion and Mesolithic Foraging', *Proceedings of the Prehistoric Society* 57 (1991): 9–14.

Mithen, S. 'The Mesolithic Age', in B. Cunliffe (ed.), *The Oxford Illustrated Prehistory of Europe*, 79–135. Oxford: Oxford University Press, 1994.

Mithen, S. (ed.). *Hunter-gatherer Landscape Archaeology. The Southern Hebrides Mesolithic Project 1988–98*. Cambridge: McDonald Institute for Archaeological Research, 2000.

Mithen, S. *After the Ice. A Global Human History 20,000–5000 BC.* London: Weidenfeld & Nicolson, 2003.

Mitrovica, J. X., M. E. Tamisiea, E. R. Ivins, L. L. A. Vermeersen, G. A. Milne and K. Lambeck. 'Surface Mass Loading on a Dynamic Earth: Complexity and Contamination in the Geodetic Analysis of Global Sea-level Trends', in J. A. Church, P. L. Woodworth, T. Aarup and W. S. Wilson (eds), *Understanding Sea-level Rise and Variability*, 285–325. Chichester: Wiley-Blackwell, 2010.

Mol, D., K. Post, J. W. F. Reumer, J. van der Plicht and J. de Vos. 'The Eurogeul – First Report of the Palaeonotological, Palynological and Archaeological Investigations of this Part of the North Sea', *Quaternary International* 142–3 (2006): 178–85.

Momber, G. 'The Inundated Landscape of the Western Solent', in N. C. Flemming (ed.), *Submarine Prehistoric Archaeology of the North Sea. Research Priorities and Collaboration with Industry*, 37–42. York: Council for British Archaeology/English Heritage (CBA Research Report 141), 2004.

Momber, G., D. Tomalin, R. Scaife, J. Satchell and J. Gillespie. *Mesolithic Occupation at Bouldnor Cliff and the Submerged Prehistoric Landscapes of the Solent.* York: Council for British Archaeology, 2011.

Mörner, N. A. 'Eustasy and Geoid Changes', *Journal of Geology* 8 (1976a): 123–51.

Mörner, N. A. 'Eustatic Changes During the Last 8,000 Years in View of Radiocarbon Calibration and New Information from the Kattegrat

Region and Other Northwestern European Coastal Areas', *Palaeography, Palaeoclimatology, and Palaeoecology* 19 (1976b): 63–85.

Morphy, H. *Ancestral Connections: Art and an Aboriginal System of Knowledge*. Chicago: University of Chicago Press, 1991.

Mortreux, C. and J. Barnett. 'Climate Change, Migration and Adaptation in Funafuti, Tuvalu', *Global Environmental Change* 19 (2009): 105–12.

Murphy, P. 'The Submerged Prehistoric Landscapes of the Southern North Sea: Work in Progress', *Landscapes* 8 (1) (2007): 1–22.

Murphy, P. *The English Coast. A History and a Prospect*. London: Continuum, 2009.

Nash, G. *A Structural Analysis of Decorated Mesolithic Artefacts from Denmark*. M.Phil thesis, University of Wales, St David's University College, 1993.

Needham, S. and C. Giardino. 'From Sicily to Salcombe: A Mediterranean Bronze Age Object from British Coastal Waters', *Antiquity* 82 (2008): 60–72.

Nelson, M. C., M. Hegmon, K. W. Kintigh, A. P. Kinzig, B. A. Nelson, J. M. Anderies, D. A. Abbott, K. A. Spielmann, S. E. Ingram, M. A. Peeples, S. Kulow, C. A. Strawhacker and C. Meegan. 'Long-term Vulnerability and Resilience: Three Examples from Archaeological Study in the Southwestern United States and Northern Mexico', in J. Cooper and P. Sheets (eds), *Surviving Sudden Environmental Change. Answers from Archaeology*, 197–221. Boulder, CO: Colorado University Press, 2012.

Nicholls, R. J. 'Impacts of and Responses to Sea-level Rise', in J. A. Church, P. L. Woodworth, T. Aarup and W. S. Wilson (eds), *Understanding Sea-level Rise and Variability*, 17–51. Chichester: Wiley-Blackwell, 2010.

Nicholls, R. J. and S. P. Leatherman. 'Global Sea-level Rise', in K. Strzepek and J. B. Smith (eds), *As Climate Changes: Potential Impacts and Implications*, 92–123. Cambridge: Cambridge University Press, 1995.

Nicholls, R. J., P. P. Wong, V. R. Burkett, J. O. Codignotto, J. E. Hay, R. F. McLean, S. Ragoonaden and C. D. Woodroffe. 'Coastal Systems and Low-lying Areas', in M. L. Parry, O. F. Canziani, J. P. Palutikof, P. J. van der Linden and C. E. Hanson (eds), *Climate Change 2007: Impacts, Adaptation and Vulnerability. Contribution of Working Group II to the*

Fourth Assessment Report of the Intergovernmental Panel on Climate Change, 315–56. Cambridge: Cambridge University Press, 2007.

Noë, A. *Out of Our Heads. Why You Are Not Your Brain, and Other Lessons From the Biology of Consciousness*. New York: Hill and Wang, 2009.

Osler, A. 'North Sea Contacts: AD 1300–1900, a Short Six Hundred Years', in C. Waddington and K. Pedersen (eds), *Mesolithic Studies in the North Sea Basin and Beyond. Proceedings of a Conference Held at Newcastle in 2003*, 12–15. Oxford: Oxbow Books, 2007.

Oxley, I. 'Constructive Conservation in England's Waters', in N. C. Flemming (ed.), *Submarine Prehistoric Archaeology of the North Sea. Research Priorities and Collaboration with Industry*, 95–8. York: Council for British Archaeology/English Heritage (CBA Research Report 141), 2004.

Palmer, S. *Mesolithic Cultures of Britain*. Poole: Dolphin Press, 1977.

Palmer, S. 'Mesolithic Sites of Portland and Their Significance', in C. Bonsall (ed.), *The Mesolithic in Europe: Proceedings of the Third International Symposium, Edinburgh 1985*, 254–7. Edinburgh: John Donald, 1989.

Palmer, S. *Culverwell Mesolithic Habitation Site, Isle of Portland, Dorset: Excavation Report and Research Studies*. Oxford: British Archaeological Reports (BAR British Series 287), 1999.

PALSEA. 'The Sea-level Conundrum: Case Studies from Palaeo-archives', *Journal of Quaternary Science* 25 (2010): 19–25.

Parker, R. *Men of Dunwich. The Story of a Vanished Town*. London: Paladin Books, 1980.

Passmore, D. G. and C. Waddington. *Archaeology and Environment in Northumberland. Till–Tweed Studies Volume II*. Oxford: Oxbow Books, 2012.

Patz, J. A., D. Campbell-Lendrum, T. Holloway and J. A. Foley. 'Impact of Regional Climate Change on Human Health', *Nature* 438 (2005): 310–17.

Pearce, F. *With Speed and Violence. Why Scientists Fear Tipping Points in Climate Change*. Boston: Beacon Press, 2007.

Pedersen, L., A. Fischer and B. Aaby. *The Danish Storebaelt Since the Ice Age: Man, Sea and Forest*. Copenhagen: A/S Storebaelt Fixed Link, 1997.

Peeters, H. 'Sites, Landscapes and Uncertainty: On the Modelling of the

Archaeological Potential and Assessment of Deeply-buried Stone Age Landscapes in the Flevoland Polders (The Netherlands)', in E. Rensink and H. Peeters (eds), *Preserving the Early Past: Investigation, Selection and Preservation of Palaeolithic and Mesolithic Sites and Landscapes*, 167–83. Amersfoort: Rijksdienst voor het Oudheidkundig Bodermonderzoek, 2006.

Peeters, H. *Hoge Vaart-A27 in Context: Towards a Model of Mesolithic-Neolithic Land Use Dynamics as a Framework for Archaeological Heritage Management*. Amersfoort, The Netherlands: Rijksdienst voor Archeologie, Cultuurlandschap en Monumenten, 2007.

Peeters, H., P. Murphy and N. C. Flemming (eds). *North Sea Prehistory Research and Management Framework (NSPRMF)*. Amersfoort: Rijksdienst voor het Cultureel Erfgoed/English Heritage, 2009.

Peltier, W. R. 'Ice Age Palaeotopography', *Science* 265 (1994): 195–201.

Peltier, W. R. 'Postglacial Variations in the Level of the Sea: Implications for Climate Dynamics and Solid-earth Geophysics', *Reviews of Geophysics* 36 (1998): 603–89.

Peltier, W. R. 'Global Glacial Isostatic Adjustment: Palaeogeodetic and Space-geodetic Tests of the ICE-4G (VM2) Model', *Journal of Quaternary Science* 17 (5–6) (2002): 491–510.

Petersen, E. B. 'Vaenget Nord: Excavation, Documentation and Interpretation of a Mesolithic Site at Vedbaek, Denmark', in C. Bonsall (ed.), *The Mesolithic in Europe: Proceedings of the Third International Symposium, Edinburgh 1985*, 325–30. Edinburgh: John Donald, 1989.

Pitts, M. 'A Gazetteer of Mesolithic Finds on the West Sussex Coastal Plain', *Sussex Archaeological Collections* 118 (1980): 153–62.

Pitts, M. and R. M. Jacobi. 'Some Aspects of Change in Flaked Stone Industries of the Mesolithic and Neolithic in Southern Britain', *Journal of Archaeological Science* 6 (1979): 163–77.

Pollard, T. 'Time and Tide: Coastal Environments, Cosmology and Ritual Practice in Early Prehistoric Scotland', in T. Pollard and A. Morrison (eds), *The Early Prehistory of Scotland*, 198–212. Edinburgh: Edinburgh University Press, 1996.

Price, T. D. 'Affluent Foragers of Southern Scandinavia', in T. D. Price and J. A. Brown (eds), *Prehistoric Hunter-gatherers: The Emergence of*

Cultural Complexity, 341–60. Orlando: Academic Press (Studies in Archaeology), 1985.

Price, T. D. 'The Mesolithic of Western Europe', *Journal of World Prehistory* 1 (3) (1987): 225–305.

Radovanović, I. *The Iron Gates Mesolithic*. Ann Arbor, MI: International Monographs in Prehistory (Archaeological Series 11), 1996.

Rankine, W. F. 'A Mesolithic Site at Farnham', *Surrey Archaeological Collections* 44 (1936): 25–46.

Rankine, W. F. 'Some Remarkable Flints from West Surrey Mesolithic Sites', *Surrey Archaeological Collections* 49 (1948): 1–14.

Rankine, W. F. 'Mesolithic Chipping Floors in the Wind-blown Deposits of West Surrey', *Surrey Archaeological Collections* 50 (1949a): 1–8.

Rankine, W. F. 'A Mesolithic Survey of the West Surrey Greensand', *Surrey Archaeological Society Research Papers* 2 (1949b): 50.

Reid, C. *Submerged Forests*. Cambridge: Cambridge University Press, 1913.

Rensink, E. and H. Peeters (eds). *Preserving the Early Past: Investigation, Selection and Preservation of Palaeolithic and Mesolithic Sites and Landscapes*. Amersfoort: Rijksdienst voor het Oudheidkundig Bodermonderzoek, 2006.

Reynier, M. *Early Mesolithic Britain. Origins, Developments and Directions*. Oxford: British Archaeological Reports (BAR British Series 393), 2005.

Rieck, F. 'Denmark', in U. Djerw and J. Rönnby (eds), *Treasures of the Baltic Sea: A Hidden Wealth of Culture*, 54–67. Stockholm: Swedish Maritime Museum, 2003.

Roberts, P. and S. Trow. *Taking to the Water: English Heritage's Initial Policy for the Management of Maritime Archaeology in England*. Swindon: English Heritage, 2002.

Rowley-Conwy, P. 'Mesolithic Danish Bacon: Permanent and Temporary Sites in the Danish Mesolithic', in A. Sheridan and G. Bailey (eds), *Economic Archaeology: Towards and Integration of Ecological and Social Approaches*, 51–65. Oxford: British Archaeological Report (BAR International Series 96), 1981.

Rowley-Conwy, P. 'The Laziness of Short-distance Hunters: The Origins of Agriculture in Western Denmark', *Journal of Anthropological Archaeology* 4 (1984): 300–24.

Rowley-Conwy, P. and M. Zvelebil. 'Saving it for Later: Storage by Prehistoric Hunter-gatherers in Europe', in P. Halstead and J. O'Shea (eds), *Bad Year Economics. Cultural Responses to Risk and Uncertainty*, 40–56. Cambridge: Cambridge University Press, 1989.

Rumsey, A. 'The Dreaming, Human Agency and Inscriptive Practice', *Oceania* 65 (2) (1994): 116–30.

Rydgren, K. and S. Bondevik. 'Moss growth patterns and timing of human exposure to a Mesolithic tsunami in the North Atlantic'. *Geology* 43 (2) (2015): 111–14.

Sainty, J. E. 'A Flaking Site on Kelling Heath, Norfolk', *Proceedings of the Prehistoric Society of East Anglia* 4 (1924): 165–76.

Sakakibara, C. '"No Whale, No Music": Inupiaq Drumming and Global Warming', *Polar Record* 45 (235) (2009): 289–303.

Sallares, R. 'Role of Environmental Changes in the Spread of Malaria in Europe During the Holocene', *Quaternary International* 150 (2006): 21–7.

Samson, A. 'Offshore Finds From the Bronze Age in North-western Europe: The Shipwreck Scenario Revisited', *Oxford Journal of Archaeology* 25 (4) (2006): 371–88.

Sarmaja-Korjonen, K. 'Correlation of Fluctuations in Cladoceran Planktonic: Littoral Ratio Between Three Cores From a Small Lake in Southern Finland: Holocene Water-level Changes', *The Holocene* 11 (2001): 53–63.

Saville, A. 'Review', *European Journal of Archaeology* 12 (1–3) (2009): 247–50.

Schmitt, L., S. Larsson, C. Schrum, I. Alekseeva, M. Tomczak and K. Svedhage. '"Why They Came"; The Colonization of the Coast of Western Sweden and its Environmental Context at the End of the Last Glaciation', *Oxford Journal of Archaeology* 25 (1) (2006): 1–28.

Schulting, R. J. 'Antlers, Bone Pins and Flint Blades: The Mesolithic Cemeteries of Téviec and Hoëdic, Brittany', *Antiquity* 70 (268) (1996): 335–50.

Schulting, R. J. *Slighting the Sea: The Mesolithic–Neolithic Transition in Northwest Europe*. PhD thesis, University of Reading, 1998.

Scudder, T. and M. Habbob. 'Aswan High Dam Resettlement', 2008. Available from www.nubian-forum.com/ (accessed 11/02/2013).

Shennan, I. 'Holocene Sea-level Changes in the North Sea Region', in I. Shennan and M. J. Tooley (eds), *Holocene Sea-level Changes in the North Sea Region*, 109–51. Oxford: Blackwell, 1987.

Shennan, I. 'Holocene Crustal Movements and Sea-level Changes in Great Britain', *Journal of Quaternary Science* 4 (1989): 77–89.

Shennan, I. and J. E. Andrews. *Holocene Land–Sea Interaction and Environmental Change Around the North Sea*. London: Geological Society (Geological Society of London Special Publication 166), 2000.

Shennan, I. and B. Horton. 'Holocene Land- and Sea-level Changes in Great Britain', *Journal of Quaternary Science* 17 (5–6) (2002): 511–26.

Shennan, I., K. Lambeck, R. Flather, B. P. Horton, J. McArthur, J. B. Innes, J. Lloyd, M. Rutherford and R. Kingfield. 'Modelling Western North Sea Palaeogeographies and Tidal Changes During the Holocene', in I. Shennan and J. Andrews (eds), *Holocene Land–Ocean Interaction and Environmental Change Around the North Sea*, 299–319. London: Geological Society of London, 2000.

Shennan, I., S. Bradley, G. Milne, A. Brooks, S. Bassett and S. Hamilton. 'Relative Sea-level Changes, Glacial Isostatic Modelling and Ice-sheet Reconstructions from the British Isles Since the Last Glacial Maximum', *Journal of Quaternary Science* 21 (6) (2006): 585–99.

Shennan, I., G. Milne and S. Bradley. 'Late Holocene Vertical Land Motion and Relative Sea-level Changes: Lessons From the British Isles', *Journal of Quaternary Science* 27 (1) (2012): 64–70.

Sievers, K. *Predicting Ecological Impacts of Climate Change and Species Introductions on a Temperate Chalk Stream in Southern Britain – A Dynamic Food Web Model Approach*. PhD thesis, Bournemouth University, 2012.

Simmons, I. G. *The Environmental Impact of Later Mesolithic Cultures: The Creation of a Moorland Landscape in England and Wales*. Edinburgh: Edinburgh University Press, 1996.

Simmons, I. G., G. W. Dimbleby and C. Grigson. 'The Mesolithic', in I. Simmons and M. Tooley (eds), *The Environment in British Prehistory*, 82–124. London: Duckworth, 1981.

Smith, A. G., A. Whittle, E. W. Cloutman and L. A. Morgan. 'Mesolithic and Neolithic Activity and Environmental Impact on the South-east

Fen-edge in Cambridgeshire', *Proceedings of the Prehistoric Society* 55 (1989): 207–49.

Smith, C. *Late Stone Age Hunters of the British Isles*. London: Routledge, 1992.

Smith, C. 'Ancestors, Place and People: Social Landscape in Aboriginal Australia', in P. J. Ucko and R. Layton (eds), *The Archaeology and Anthropology of Landscape*, 189–205. Abingdon: Routledge, 1999.

Smith, D. E., R. A. Cullingford and B. A. Haggart. 'A Major Coastal Flood During the Holocene in Eastern Scotland', *Eiszeitalter und Gegenwart* 35 (1985): 109–18.

Smith, D. E., S. Shi, R. Cullingford, A. Dawson, C. Firth, I. Foster, P. Fretwell, B. Haggart, L. Holloway and D. Long. 'The Holocene Storegga Slide Tsunami in the United Kingdom', *Quaternary Science Reviews* 23 (2004): 2291–311.

Souffi, B. *Le Mésolithique en Haute-Normandie (France). L'example du site d'Acquigny 'L'Onglais' (Eure) et sa Contribution à l'étude des Gisements Mésolithiques de Plein Air*. Oxford: British Archaeological Reports (BAR International 1307), 2004.

Souffi, B. 'Le Mesolithique de Haute Normandie: Taphonomie et Interpretation Chronoculturelle', in J-P. Fagnart, A. Thevenin, T. Ducrocq, B. Souffi and P. Coudret (eds), *Le Début du Mésolithique en Europe du Nord-Ouest*, 135–52. Paris: Mémoires de la Société Préhistorique Française 45, 2008.

Spikins, P. *Mesolithic Northern England: Environment, Population and Settlement*. Oxford: British Archaeological Reports (BAR British Series 283), 1999.

Steffen, K., R. H. Thomas, E. Rignot, J. G. Cogley, M. B. Dyurgerov, S. C. B. Raper, P. Huybrechts and E. Hanna. 'Cryospheric Contributions to Sea-level Rise and Variability', in J. A. Church, P. L. Woodworth, T. Aarup and W. S. Wilson (eds), *Understanding Sea-level Rise and Variability*, 177–225. Chichester: Wiley-Blackwell, 2010.

Strassburg, J. *Shamanic Shadows. One Hundred Generations of Undead Subversion in Southern Scandinavia 7,000–4,000 BC*. Stockholm: Stockholm University (Studies in Archaeology 20), 2000.

Sturges, W. and B. G. Hong. 'Decadal Variability of Sea-level', in

B. C. Douglas, M. S. Kearney and S. P. Leatherman (eds), *Sea-level Rise. History and Consequences*, 165–80. London Academic Press (International Geophysics Series 75), 2001.

Sturt, F. 'Local Knowledge is Required: A Rhythmanalytical Approach to the Late Mesolithic and Early Neolithic of the East Anglian Fenland, UK', *Journal of Maritime Archaeology* 1 (2006): 119–39.

Tappin, D. R., B. Pearce, S. Fitch, D. Dove, B. Gearey, J. M. Hill, C. Chambers, R. Bates, J. Pinnion, D. Diaz Doce, M. Green, J. Gallyot, L. Georgiou, D. Brutto, S. Marzialetti, E. Hopla, E. Ramsay and H. Fielding. *The Humber Regional Environmental Characterisation*. British Geological Survey Open Report OR/10/54, 2011.

Taylor, J. 'A Burnt Mesolithic Hunting Camp on the Mendips: A Preliminary Report on Structural Traces Excavated on Lower Pitts Farm, Priddy, Somerset', in S. Milliken and J. Cook (eds), *A Very Remote Period Indeed*, 260–7. Oxford: Oxford University Press, 2001.

Thibault, K. M. and J. H. Brown. 'Impact of an Extreme Climatic Event on Community Assembly', *Proceedings of the National Academy of Sciences of the United States of America* 105 (9) (2008): 3410–15.

Thomas, E. R., E. W. Wolff, R. Mulvaney, J. P. Steffensen, S. J. Johnsen, C. Arrowsmith, J. W. C. White, B. Vaughn and T. Popp. 'The 8.2 kyr Event from Greenland Ice Cores', *Quaternary Science Reviews* 26 (1–2) (2007): 70–81.

Thorpe, I. J. N. 'Death and Violence – The Later Mesolithic of Southern Scandinavia', in L. Bevan and J. Moore (eds), *Peopling the Mesolithic in a Northern Environment*, 171–80. Oxford: Archaeopress (BAR International Series 1157), 2003.

Thorpe, N., S. Eyegetok, N. Hakongak and the Kitikmeot Elders. 'Nowadays it is Not the Same: Inuit Qaujimajatuqangit, Climate and Caribou in the Kitikmeot Region of Nunavut, Canada', in I. Krupnik and D. Jolly (eds), *The Earth is Faster Now: Indigenous Observations of Arctic Environmental Change*, 198–239. Fairbanks, AK: Arctic Research Consortium of the United States, 2002.

Tipping, R. 'Interpretive Issues Concerning the Driving Forces of Vegetation Change in the Early Holocene of the British Isles', in A. Saville (ed.), *Mesolithic Scotland and its Neighbours: The Early Holocene*

Prehistory of Scotland, its British and Irish Context, and Some Northern Perspectives, 45–54. Edinburgh: Society of Antiquaries of Scotland, 2004.

Tipping, R. and E. Tisdall. 'Continuity, Crisis and Climate Change in the Neolithic and Early Bronze Periods of North West Europe', in I. A. G. Shepherd and G. Barclay (eds), *Scotland in Ancient Europe. The Neolithic and Early Bronze Age of Scotland in their European Context*, 71–82. Edinburgh: Society of Antiquaries of Scotland, 2004.

Tipping, R., P. Ashmore, A. Davies, B. A. Haggart, A. Moir, A. Newton, R. Sands, T. Skinner and E. Tisdall. 'Prehistoric *Pinus* Woodland Dynamics in an Upland Landscape in Northern Scotland: The Roles of Climate Change and Human Impact', *Vegetation History and Archaeobotany* 17 (2008): 251–67.

Togola, T. 'Memories, Abstractions, and Conceptualization of Ecological Crisis in the Mande World', in R. J. McIntosh, J. A. Tainter and S. K. McIntosh (eds), *The Way the Wind Blows. Climate, History, and Human Action*, 181–92. New York: Columbia University Press, 2000.

Tooley, M. J. *Sea-level Changes: Northwest England During the Flandrian Stage*. Oxford: Clarendon Press, 1978.

Tooley, M. J. 'Sea-levels', *Progress in Physical Geography* 9 (1985): 113–20.

Torry, W. 'Natural Disasters, Social Structure and Change in Traditional Societies', *Journal of Asian and African Studies* 13 (3/4) (1978): 167–83.

Turney, C. S. M. and H. Brown. 'Catastrophic Early Holocene Sea-level Rise, Human Migration and the Neolithic Transition in Europe', *Quaternary Science Reviews* 26 (2007): 2036–41.

Uldum, O. C. 'The Excavation of a Mesolithic Double Burial From Tybrind Vig, Denmark', in J. Benjamin, C. Bonsall, C. Pickard and A. Fischer (eds), *Submerged Prehistory*, 15–20. Oxford: Oxbow Books, 2011.

Van de Noort, R. *North Sea Archaeologies. A Maritime Biography 10,000 BC–AD 1500*. Oxford: Oxford University Press, 2011.

Verhart, L. B. M. 'The Implications of Prehistoric Finds On and Off the Dutch Coast', in N. C. Flemming (ed.), *Submarine Prehistoric Archaeology of the North Sea. Research Priorities and Collaboration with Industry*, 57–61. York: Council for British Archaeology/English Heritage (CBA Research Report 141), 2004.

Verjux, C. 'The Function of the Mesolithic Sites in the Paris Basin (France). New Data', in L. Larsson, H. Kindgren, K. Knutsson, D. Loeffler and A. Åkerlund (eds), *Mesolithic on the Move*, 262–8. Oxford: Oxbow Books, 2003.

Vink, A., H. Steffen, L. Reinhardt and G. Kaufmann. 'Holocene Relative Sea-level Change, Isostatic Subsidence and the Radial Viscosity Structure of the Mantle of Northwest Europe (Belgium, The Netherlands, Germany, Southern North Sea)', *Quaternary Science Reviews* 26 (2007): 3249–75.

Voytek, B. and R. Tringham. 'Rethinking the Mesolithic: The Case of South-east Europe', in C. Bonsall (ed.), *The Mesolithic in Europe: Proceedings of the Third International Symposium, Edinburgh 1985*, 492–9. Edinburgh: John Donald, 1989.

Waddington, C. (ed.). *Mesolithic Settlement in the North Sea Basin: A Case Study from Howick, North-East England*. Oxford: Oxbow Books and English Heritage, 2007.

Waddington, C. and K. Pedersen (eds). *Mesolithic Studies in the North Sea Basin and Beyond. Proceedings of a Conference Held at Newcastle in 2003*. Oxford: Oxbow Books, 2007.

Wagner, B., O. Bennike, M. Klug and H. Cremer. 'First Indication of Storegga Tsunami Deposits from East Greenland', *Journal of Quaternary Science* 22 (4) (2007): 321–5.

Ward, I., P. Larcombe and M. Lillie. 'The Dating of Doggerland – Post-glacial Geochronology of the Southern North Sea', *Environmental Archaeology* 11 (2) (2006): 207–18.

Weninger, B., R. Schulting, M. Bradtmoller, L. Clare, M. Collard, K. Edinborough, J. Hilpert, O. Joris, M. Niekus, E. J. Rohling and B. Wagner. 'The Catastrophic Final Flooding of Doggerland by the Storegga Slide Tsunami', *Documenta Praehistorica* 35 (2008): 1–24.

Wessex Archaeology. *Seabed Prehistory: Gauging the Effects of Marine Aggregate Dredging. Round 2. Final Report. Volume VIII: Ref. 57422.17.* Salisbury: Wessex Archaeology, 2007.

Wessex Archaeology. *Seabed Prehistory: Gauging the Effects of Marine Aggregate Dredging. Round 2 Final Report, Volume I: Introduction.* Unpublished English Heritage MALSF project, 2008a.

Wessex Archaeology. *Seabed Prehistory: Gauging the Effects of Marine Aggregate Dredging. Round 2, Final Report, Volume II: Arun.* Unpublished English Heritage MALSF project, 2008b.

Wessex Archaeology. *Seabed Prehistory: Gauging the Effects of Marine Aggregate Dredging. Final Report, Round 2, Volume III: Arun Additional Grabbing.* Unpublished English Heritage MALSF project, 2008c.

Westwood, J. and J. Simpson. *The Lore of the Land. A Guide to England's Legends, From Spring-heeled Jack to the Witches of Warboys.* London: Penguin Books, 2005.

Wheeler, M. *Archaeology From the Earth.* Harmondsworth: Penguin, 1954.

Woodman, P. C. *Excavations at Mount Sandel 1973-77.* Belfast: Her Majesty's Stationery Office (Northern Ireland Archaeological Monographs 2), 1985.

Wymer, J. J. *Gazetteer of Mesolithic Sites in England and Wales.* London: Council for British Archaeology (CBA Research Report 20), 1977.

Yarrow, T. 'Kinship and the Core House: Contested Understandings of Kinship and Place in a Ghanaian Resettlement Township', in J. Edwards and M. Petrović-Šteger (eds), *Recasting Anthropological Knowledge: Inspiration and Social Science*, 88-105. Cambridge: Cambridge University Press, 2011.

Yu, S-Y., B. E. Berglund, P. Sandgren and K. Lambeck. 'Evidence for a Rapid Sea-level Rise 7600yr Ago', *Geology* 35 (10) (2007): 891-4.

Zvelebil, M. 'Mesolithic Societies and the Transition to Farming: Problems of Time, Scale and Organisation', in M. Zvelebil (ed.), *Hunters in Transition: Mesolithic Societies and Their Transition to Farming*, 167-88. Cambridge: Cambridge University Press, 1986.

Zvelebil, M. 'Economic Intensification and Postglacial Hunter-gatherers in North Temperate Europe', in C. Bonsall (ed.), *The Mesolithic in Europe: Proceedings of the Third International Symposium, Edinburgh 1985*, 80-8. Edinburgh: John Donald, 1989.

Zvelebil, M. 'People Behind the Lithics. Social Life and Social Conditions of Mesolithic Communities in Temperate Europe', in L. Bevan and J. Moore (eds), *Peopling the Mesolithic in a Northern Environment*, 1-26. Oxford: British Archaeological Report (BAR International Series 1157), 2003.

Zvelebil, M. 'Mobility, Contact, and Exchange in the Baltic Sea Basin 6000–2000 BC', *Journal of Anthropological Archaeology* 25 (2006): 178–92.

Zvelebil, M. 'Rite, Ritual, and Materiality of Information in Mesolithic Europe', in R. Whallon, W. A. Lovis and R. K. Hitchcock (eds), *Information and its Role in Hunter-gatherer Bands*, 181–201. Los Angeles, CA: Cotsen Institute of Archaeology Press (Ideas, Debates and Perspectives 5), 2011.

Zwally, H. J., W. Abdalati, T. Herring, K. Larson, J. Saba and K. Steffen. 'Surface Melt-induced Acceleration of Greenland Ice-sheet Flow', *Science* 297 (2002): 218–22.

Index